TEACH YOURSELF HORSE

NATURAL HORSE MANAGEMENT

HEATHER SIMPSON

A HORSE'S MOUTH PUBLICATION

First published in Great Britain in 2004
D J Murphy (Publishers) Ltd
The Horse's Mouth is an imprint of
D J Murphy (Publishers) Ltd

Text: **Heather Simpson**

Editor: **Janet Rising**
Designer: **Jamie Powell**
Published by: **D J Murphy (Publishers) Ltd**
Headley House, Headley Road, Grayshott, Surrey GU26 6TU
Origination by: **Ford Graphics Ltd**, Ringwood, Hampshire
Printed by: **Wyndeham Grange**, Brighton, West Sussex.

ISBN 0-9513707-8-2

Photography credits
All photographs at the Natural Animal Centre by **Bob Atkins.**
Photography on pages 50, 56, 113 and 122 by **Bob Atkins.**
Photography on pages 24, 25, 51, 61, 64-73,
75, 77, 80, 81, 83, 85, 88, 89, 91 by **Bob Langrish.**
Photography on pages 40, 41, 50, 55, 87, 90, 94, 111
and 121 **D J Murphy Library.**
Front cover image by **Bob Langrish.**
Eohippus artwork on page 16 by **Dianne Breeze.**
Horse's Mouth logo by **Anne Pilgrim.**

CONTENTS

PREFACE

In the mid-Nineties, I eagerly returned to university for the fourth time in my life – this time to attain another post-graduate degree which would give me the scientific knowledge to work with horses and other animals that had behavioural problems. But although my academic studies certainly fulfilled this goal, I soon realised that the practical skill needed to help horses from a scientific perspective was something I was, to a large extent, going to have to develop myself. Certainly, I only wished to use techniques in line with the Natural Animal Centre philosophy of how horses should be treated – with fairness, dignity and integrity.

By 1997, I was dreaming of ways to help horse owners gain access to the science of horse behaviour and with the formal launch of the Equine Behaviour Qualification (the EBQ) in 2000 followed in 2001, by the launch of *Positive Horse Magic*, a positive reinforcement horse training system devised by my husband Ross and myself, my dream had finally become a reality.

You will not find anything new in terms of equine behavioural theory in the following pages. All I hope to have achieved is to extract some of the most salient aspects of this discipline for horse owners, and give it more accessibility than is usually found in the average textbook or science journal.

However, the practical application of some of the scientific theories – particularly those outlined at the end of chapters and in the detail of Part Three – are indeed my own.

With *Positive Horse Magic* too, Ross and I have never claimed originality. Positive reinforcement has been around for as long as man; indeed, behavioural psychologist Thorndike scientifically proved its existence in 1911. But like the EBQ, Positive Horse Magic was born because we wanted to help horse owners explore the awesome possibilities positive reinforcement training can offer. And when it comes to solving horse behavioural problems, positive reinforcement brings an exciting, all-encompassing dimension in developing the relationship between horse and owner for the better.

At the Natural Animal Centre, the principles of the EBQ and *Positive Horse Magic* are a living concept, as many of the chapters in this book will testify.

I sincerely hope that this volume of *Teach Yourself Horse* brings you as much enjoyment, fun and pure magic as I have had in writing it.

Heather Simpson

INTRODUCTION TO TEACH YOURSELF HORSE

The monthly *Teach Yourself Horse* series first appeared in *Horse& Rider* magazine in July 2001. As it gained in popularity, readers often requested two things: that the series be converted into a handier form, and that it be written in such a way that it could be used as a self-study guide. As the Equine Behaviour Qualification at the Natural Animal Centre also gained popularity, it became clear to me that, despite the extensive reading list which EBQ students are required to plod their way through, one more text was still needed; one that would incorporate the essence of solving horse behaviour problems as presented in the EBQ. And so the idea for this book was born.

You will see that each chapter comprises:

■ Sections on equine behavioural or learning theory (as the scientists currently know it).

■ Questions which are set out at the beginning. These can be used in the manner of self-study. After you have read a chapter, use the questions to test yourself to see if you've understood what you have read. If you are unable to answer some questions, you will need to re-read the chapter; the answers will always be buried in that particular chapter.

■ Photographs that are a pictorial representation of both the theoretical and practical aspects which are being presented.

■ At least two or three practical ideas (some chapters have many more) for you to try out with your own horse.

In this way, you will get the most out of Teach Yourself Horse!

PART ONE

CHAPTER ONE

GROUP LIVING

After reading this chapter, you should be able to answer questions on the following:

- When horses were first domesticated
- Why horses choose to live in a group
- Why horses pair-bond and how they choose a pair-bond
- Which horse leads the herd
- Why horses should not be kept on their own
- Whether it is acceptable to mix mares and geldings together
- Why turning a horse out with the same horses every day is important
- How to break the tedium for a horse on box rest

Have you ever stopped to think that your horse actually lives in a world of two societies? The first is the one he shares with human beings and the other, more secret one, is his life with other horses.

You probably know a lot about your horse when he interacts with you and other people, but how much do you really know about what happens in your horse's life when you're not around? Do you really know what motivates him? Are you really sure you know what his needs are and, if you were able to ask him, would his answer be the same as yours? You may think that you are already taking care of your horse's needs – you exercise him regularly, you give him a clean, dry stable with a lovely warm bed, you feed him a well-known recommended food with plenty of good-quality hay and give him the best veterinary attention

Your horse enjoys a secret life with his peers. . .

. . . as well as the life he shares with human beings.

whenever necessary. But is this enough from your horse's point of view?

In this book I will be bringing you some new, interesting information about why horses do what they do. More importantly, I will also be providing you with a number of practical ideas on how to positively use this knowledge to improve the quality of your horse's life.

So read on!

Safety in numbers

Horses like to live in herds because, as prey animals, they find safety in being in a group.

The biological motivation for this strategy is simple: if there are predators around, being part of a group means it is more likely that an individual horse will survive to live another day. The more eyes, ears and noses there are around to sense danger, the better chance the herd has of not being targeted.

In behavioural studies, scientists discovered that groups of starlings, birds which also like to live in large numbers, were able to spend more time eating and were quicker to respond to danger than a solitary starling, which had to spend large amounts of time being vigilant and was slower in escaping from a threat.

Friends for life

There are, of course, many species of prey animals that like to live in herds, like zebras and antelope. But horses are special, in that they also pair-bond. Most importantly as horse owners, we should be aware that without human interference, horses pair-bond for life.

In the wild, horses will mutually select each other and will usually choose a partner that is the same age, sex and size as themselves. Where they are unable to find the 'ideal' pair-bond, however, they will look for the next best thing. The biological purpose of the pair-bonding drive is that the horse not only has the protection of the herd, but also a special friend to watch over him, as well as someone to eat alongside, to play with and to groom.

True-life experiences

At the Natural Animal Centre, we have taken in a number of rescue horses, the majority of which have come from rescue centres. Most of the horses have pair-bonded as described earlier, but there is one pair that truly breaks the rule – a 13-year-old, 17.1hh Cleveland Bay gelding, Troy, has bonded with a seven-year-old, 13hh pony, Panda.

Panda came to us at the age of four months when he was found starving in a field with two very old Highland ponies – there was no sign of Panda's mother, there was no grazing and all three had been completely neglected. Not only had they not been fed, they were also infested with lice and worms, and the hooves of the older two looked like they had not been trimmed for months.

For the first two years of Panda's life at the NAC, he showed signs of pairing with a young filly his age and size. But when the herd leader died, Troy took on the mantle of leadership and at the same time demonstrated an obvious parental role over the two youngsters. As the months went by, this role began to change and Troy and Panda now have the strongest pair-bond of any twosome in the herd.

One of the reasons such an unlikely duo occurred is that both horses were suffering a significant loss – Panda had lost his mother very early in life and had not fully settled down in his new herd, and Troy had just lost his pair-bond (and herd leader). By pairing, they fulfilled each other's needs and the association ultimately grew into the more usual pair-bond relationship.

At the Natural Animal Centre, Panda and Troy have formed a strong pair-bond due to their shared circumstances.

A TIME OF CHANGE . . .

Sixty five million years ago, an animal not much bigger than a cat roamed the earth, spending most of its time in forests and woodlands. This animal was called Eohippus (left), the ancestor of the horse we know today.

When we start learning about how horses behave naturally, it is important to remember that only 12,000 years ago – a mere blink of an equine eyelid on the evolutionary scale – horses were being kept exclusively for the purposes of being eaten by people. And it is only around 2,000 years ago that we find the first evidence of horses being ridden, because the skulls of these ancient horses show damage to the horse's jaw through the use of harsh bits.

But the biggest change came about 100 years ago with the increase in the use of mechanised machinery. For the first time, the horse became largely redundant for work and was kept solely for recreational purposes.

Today, we live in a world where it is common to see horses without focus or function, in which they are kept singly with very little turnout and barely adequate physical exercise. Often, the emotional needs of the horse are only partially addressed and where some owners talk of behaviour problems in horses, in reality, abnormal behaviours can occur merely because horses are straining to adapt to the modern ways in which they are managed.

Once you start to realise that it is possible to allow your horse to act out many of his natural behaviours in a domestic setting, then you are well on the way to having a problem-free, relaxed and happy horse.

SEXUAL POLITICS

Under natural circumstances, contrary to the macho image of the stallion, it is in fact a lead mare that takes charge of the herd. Horses belong to a select group of animals which live in a matriarchal society – as do elephants! The alpha mare decides where and when the herd will move, when it is time to drink and when it is safe to doze. Both geldings and mares benefit from being in a mixed group because of the enriched social life. The prime urge of the stallion is not herd leadership, but sexual reproduction and he is motivated by trying to transfer his genes through mating with as many mares as possible.

The alpha mare decides when the herd will move - and the other horses follow her lead.

Keeping horses happy

It may be necessary to keep your horse confined – in box rest, for example, but you can still make his life more fulfiled. He needs to recuperate physically, but don't ignore his mental and emotional needs.

■ **Social contact.** If he already has a pair-bond, make sure they are stabled next to each other at nights, so that your horse has his favourite company for at least part of the day. During the day, bring his pair-bond up from the field for short visits. Allow them to smell each other and nuzzle over the stable door. Even if your horse is not pair-bonded, you can still bring equine visitors to his stable, particularly those that are part of his regular turnout group.

■ **Frequent feeder.** Divide your horse's daily food intake into four or six meals per day. By breaking up the the tedium of the day more often, your horse is much less likely to develop stable vices, particularly where he is on enforced, long-term rest for several months.

■ **Toy joy.** Giving your injured horse a toy box at least once a day helps fulfil some of his daily play needs. You can use either a cardboard apple box, or a plastic storage box. Fill the box with empty containers, such as used yogurt or fizzy drink bottles. Cut a hole in the sides of some of the bottles and place a small number of pony nuts inside. The idea is that the horse has to use his natural foraging skills to find the bottles which contain the nuts, then roll them around until they fall out and can be eaten. Add some chopped apple, carrots and parsnips, as well. Always supervise your horse's playtime with his box. Some horses attempt to eat the bottles whole; if so, it would be wise to invest in a sturdy, purpose-made horse toy.

■ **Tiny turnout.** Nearing the end of your horse's box rest, ask your vet whether you could turn him out in a small area of the field instead of a stable. This will allow him to feel more part of the social group again.

A toy box fulfils some of a horse's play needs.

So, what does the information in this chapter tell us about the care of domestic horses?

■ A horse should not be kept on its own because this could affect its emotional well-being. As a prey animal, a horse relies on the herd for shared vigilance and safety. Keeping him on his own may cause the horse to endure a life of unrelenting stress, which could lead to health problems such as gastric ulcers. Consider your horse's point of view by making sure he always has equine companionship – by doing so, you will fulfil one of his greatest needs in life.

■ It is perfectly acceptable for mares and geldings to graze together, as both sexes do naturally and happily in the wild. Horses are highly social animals and having access to others of either sex and varying ages allows them to become more well-rounded psychologically.

■ It is important to turn your horse out with the same horses every day. Allowing your horse to be part of a regular herd gives him the best possible chance of finding a pair-bond and fulfilling his most fundamental needs. It also gives the herd the opportunity for a herd leader to emerge – an important factor in how horses cope with danger. Apart from your horse's own sense of well-being, the more permanent and stable the herd population and structure, the calmer and safer all the horses will be. The most common reason people give for not turning their horse out in a group is fear of injury, but such fears usually prove groundless where horses are allowed to live in a permanent group.

Allowing your horse to become part of a regular herd is important for his mental wellbeing.

CHAPTER TWO

GROUP DYNAMICS

After reading this chapter, you should be able to answer questions on the following:

- What a linear hierarchy means
- Why the concept of a linear hierarchy in horses is flawed
- How contesting resources is crucial to establishing dominance
- Why submission is part of the dominance equation
- Why instability in a domestic yard causes fighting amongst horses
- The options open to the horse when a threat is encountered – the four F's
- How horses have different spatial perceptions
- How to introduce a new horse to an existing herd

Wild horses are surprisingly amicable toward each other most of the time, yet one of the most common reasons I am given by people refusing to turn out their horses in groups is fear of their horse getting injured – by another horse! Even if most of the horses at a yard appear fairly docile, it just takes one troublemaker to upset the peace, and the threat of injury becomes uppermost in everyone's mind. So why is this in complete contrast to the natural state, where wild horses seem to get on with each other and no injuries occur? Or is this a false, romantic notion on our part? Before we can get to the bottom of this question, there are two important principles you need to understand:

- How dominance and submission work in horses.
- How horses perceive the space around them.

Horses are not chickens!

In the Thirties, a now-famous Dutch animal behavioural scientist, Schelderupp, spent a considerable amount of time observing how hens interacted with each other. He learnt that hens arranged their social group in order of the most dominant hen to the least dominant. He called this a 'pecking order' and this social order is called a linear hierarchy ie, Hen A is dominant over Hen B who is dominant over Hen C, and so on. At the time, he seemed to have found the key to how the animal kingdom works. But behavioural scientists were soon to discover

that Schelderupp's approach was too simplistic. So it was back to the drawing board for a while until the answer was found.

Horse hierarchies and how they are formed

Horses don't simply rise to the top of the herd hierarchy by magic. To be accepted as a leader by the others and to be able to retain that leadership, the alpha horse has to be accepted as such by each individual in the herd. If a horse wants to know if it is more – or less – dominant than the next horse, it needs to test its relationship with that particular horse on a one-to-one basis. It does this by having contests with the other horse over things that are potentially valuable to both of them. For example, having access to the water trough in the field might be worth contesting because water is a life-giving resource. So, in the wild in a circumstance where there was a scarcity of water because of drought, the contest to get to the water first could be a very serious one between two horses. Using body language, facial expressions and ear and tail positions, the horses communicate to other horses to come

Although a water trough in a field may always be full, horses will assert their position in the herd by deciding who drinks first – if at all.

Horses have to win contests with other horses over all valuable resources – even controlling the amount of free space it has around it.

closer or to stay away. The one that succeeds in driving the second horse away from the water is the winner of the contest and becomes the dominant one. Or does it?

Interestingly, the story doesn't end here; the horse has only won the dominance contest with respect to access to water. It has to win contests with the same horse over many other valuable resources; the best food, having the most shade under a tree on a very hot day – even controlling the amount of free space around it. The contests go on until the one horse concedes and stops contesting. Previous experience of always losing eventually causes the one horse to simply stop trying to take on the other horse. Only at this point could you say the one horse is dominant over the other.

Having sorted out that relationship, the horse would now turn its attention to other individuals in the herd and would keep going until, one by one, the nature of dominance or submission had been ascertained between each relationship. We can, therefore, end up with a herd hierarchy where Horse A is dominant over Horse B, Horse B is dominant over Horse C but Horse C is dominant over Horse A.

The pacifists!

Of course, many animals make a decision not to get involved in dominance disputes in the first place and simply concede at the mere suggestion of a contest. Sorting out rankings in the herd is dependent therefore on age, sex and size of the individuals involved. If you are a small, one-year-old filly for example, it doesn't make sense to risk injury by challenging a large stallion; it is far more sensible to concede and survive to live another day.

Here's another important fact: the establishment of dominance relies on deference – there has to be one individual who agrees to give in, or to defer. Without this agreement of deference, horses would spend too much time and energy squabbling in the herd and they would lose condition, even die.

Why do horses at a livery yard sometimes end up fighting?

It is important to remember that when we encounter horses which are fighting at a yard, then these horses are behaving abnormally from an evolutionary perspective. The drive to form a stable hierarchy is ultimately motivated by their need for safety in numbers, so expending energy through aggression towards each other is counter-productive to that goal. Yet many livery yards run turn-out arrangements which do not support attempts by the horses to sort out the herd hierarchy. Often, they are turned out with different individuals every day and often in different fields, creating uncertainty. Thus, the need to sort out rankings and which parts of the field are valuable becomes most pressing. If hierarchies remain vague or only partially resolved, some of the horses become anxious and even *fear-aggressive*. Some may even start to show these responses immediately they are confronted with a new horse and it is this stage that the risk of aggression and injury in the group is high. The solution, however, is simple: maintain a regime where the same group of horses is turned out together every day. If the horses are all stabled overnight, there is already considerable herd disruption so, by at least allowing them to spend the day together, you have an excellent chance of the hierarchy sorting itself out peaceably.

One more factor influences the nature of dominance in horses: pair-bonds. How high an individual is ranked in a herd, may not be the same when it is with its pair-bond. So two horses can have a combined higher ranking when they are paired than when they are separated. By keeping horses in permanent, stable groups and with the right-pair bond, you will have a calmer, more peaceful herd, and the risk of injury becomes very low.

EVERY HORSE'S NEED FOR SPACE

When any animal is faced with something threatening in the environment, it has four choices of how to deal with the problem, known colloquially as the 'Four F's'. So a horse faced with a threat approaching could do one of the following:

- Stay and *Fight*.
- Try to escape from danger by taking *Flight*.
- *Freeze* on the spot and hope the danger passes.
- *Fiddle* about! This is where the animal tries to avoid confrontations by acting out appeasing behaviours which communicate to another that it does not want to get involved in an aggressive encounter.

  Sorting out dominance and submission between two individuals always involves potential fight or flight behaviours and if we curtail our horses' ability to take flight because there is not enough space, then we contribute greatly to the chances of fight responses occurring and, of course, injury.

A horse may try to escape from danger by taking flight.

The horse's three space needs

Pair-bond

Personal

Herd space

THREE DIMENSIONS

So how much space do horses need? Horses live in a number of spatial dimensions, and these three are the most important for you to know:

■ Personal space – like our own, this space can get bigger or smaller depending on the intensity of the perceived danger. Only very special individuals are invited to cross the personal space line of a horse (eg a pair-bond).

■ Pair-bond space – this surrounds a bonded pair which other horses may not enter unless invited. Again, the size of this space depends on how safe the pair feels.

■ Herd space – this is the area surrounding the herd as it moves around. In studies of some wild horses, it was found that many herds have home ranges that overlap in certain areas. So, in certain instances horses from another herd will be tolerated in the original herd's space. But as soon as the scarcity or value of something in the environment increases (eg access to water at a water hole), then a herd will defend its space by driving the others away.

Assuming the fields at a yard are not very large, how could I go about introducing a new horse into the existing herd so that the least disruption occurs?

By gradually allowing the hierarchy to adjust and re-form around the new horse. People often make the mistake of throwing a new horse into a field with the whole group present. This causes the established hierarchy to be totally disrupted as the horses go through the process of re-assessing one-to-one relationships with the new horse. The presence of a new horse can cause some to go up in rank and, of course, others to go down. The best tried-and-tested manner I have used at the Natural Animal Centre for safely introducing new horses to each other, is to have the new horse initially meet only one individual.

1. Remove a middle-ranked individual from the herd and introduce it to the new horse. You can do this by placing them both in a small field so that they are separated by a fence but can touch each other without causing injury. If things do start to get out of hand, they would both be able to take safe flight in their own field. Sometimes, such introductions take only a matter of hours for acceptance between the two to be reached – but you should be looking for the total acceptance of both horses entering each other's personal space. In this situation, horses show this by grazing as closely together as possible, and grooming each other.

2. Now you are ready to remove the physical barrier of the fence and all should proceed smoothly. Once the pair has had an opportunity to settle down together over a period of time (say, on average, one to three weeks), you are ready to introduce them both into the herd.

3. Put the pair in their herd. Because herd hierarchies vary according to which horse is pair-bonded with another, by pairing the new horse with a middle-ranked individual you have the greatest chance of the pair being accepted as approximately middle-ranked when they re-enter the group. This method typically ensures that the new horse is not automatically relegated to the bottom and it will also enjoy the protection and companionship of a special friend.

New friends; after time in adjoining fields, and then turned out in a field together, the new horse and his new, middle-ranked friend are ready to join the main herd.

Once they have had time to get used to the field together . . .

. . . they join the herd without too much disruption.

CHAPTER THREE

WHAT DO HORSES
REALLY NEED?

The idea that animals had needs, and could suffer if they weren't met, was once quite radical.

After reading this chapter, you should be able to answer questions on the following:

- The Five Freedoms as a test of animal welfare
- What the Five Freedoms are
- How your own horse's management measures up to the Five Freedoms
- The needs of the horse as behavioural scientists see them
- The priority of these needs
- How the needs work in a stable herd, such as the one based at the Natural Animal Centre

One of the first exercises students attempt when they study the Equine Behaviour Qualification (the EBQ) at the Natural Animal Centre, is to list as many needs of the horse as they can, and then work out how many of these they think are actually fulfilled in the 'average' yard in Britain today. They then have to work out which compromises horse owners could make to enable the lives of their horses to become more satisfying.

Welfare question
Understanding the needs of animals is a question that has long occupied the minds of many behavioural scientists who are involved in researching the welfare of domesticated animals. As long ago as 1965, a committee was

set up by the British Government to review the welfare of farm animals – remember this was at a time when the words organic and free range were not part of our daily vocabulary and intensive animal farming was not subject to the moral debate it is today. At that time, with the benefit of new technology and drugs, farmers were suddenly in a position where they could simultaneously farm larger numbers of animals than ever before, and so we witnessed the advent of the first battery chicken farms and the intensive stall farming of pigs and other animals. A great idea for boosting farm profits, no doubt, but not so great if you were a chicken or pig.

But, fortunately, in the middle of this rapid and fundamental change to traditional farming practices, some people began to feel uncomfortable about the welfare of these animals – hence the need for the commission to review the whole situation. The idea that any animal had 'needs' and that it 'needed' to do certain things at certain times was quite radical at the time. Indeed, the whole idea that animals could even suffer was a fairly novel thought.

Five Freedoms
In the event, the committee proved to be one of the most important ever in the field of farm animal welfare: their recommendations are now famous in the world of animal welfare. Through these recommendations – which became known as Brambell's Five Freedoms (Brambell was the man who chaired the committee) – they revolutionised the way we now look at animal needs. They recommended that, as the bare minimum, an individual animal should enjoy at the very least, the following Freedoms:

- Freedom from hunger and thirst
- Freedom from disease
- Freedom from excessive heat or excessive cold
- Freedom of movement
- Freedom to act out most normal behaviours

Your horse and the Five Freedoms
No one would suggest that the life of the horse is similar to that of the battery hen, but how well do you think your own horse really does with respect to the Five Freedoms? Consider the needs of the wild horse, and then compare your own horse's day-to-day routine with these.

You might think that you definitely keep your horse free from hunger and thirst but if he were in the wild, what would he eat, how much would he eat and for how long every day would he eat?

Rolling: a normal behaviour – one of the Five Freedoms listed.

Freedom from hunger and thirst. Are our domestic horses' needs met as they would be in the wild?

Would he drink every day? Is it the same situation for your own horse?

In the wild, a horse would eat for an average of 16 hours a day – a morning and evening feed with an accompanying haynet would not, therefore, meet his basic needs when it comes to natural feeding behaviours. On the other hand, wild horses often drink only every second day, depending on which part of the world they live, leading some behavioural scientists to think that sometimes stabled horses only drink every night because there is nothing else to do.

Is your horse really kept free from excessive heat or excessive cold?

Stand still for a couple of hours and you will probably find that you start to feel cold. With this in mind, we should try to be more aware of the temperature needs of the stabled horse, even if he wears a stable rug. How many of us could say that we have checked our horse's temperature at 4am on a regular basis during the winter months, after most horses will have been standing still for around 12 hours? At the other end of the spectrum, paddocks that have been picked clean of any shrub, bush or tree do not give the horse the ability to regulate his temperature on a hot summer's day, either.

Is your horse free to act out his normal behaviours?

If you own a gelding (as many of us do) then consider that we deny these horses the most fundamental of natural behaviours – the drive to reproduce. And what of the mares that repeatedly come into season with all the accompanying desires to reproduce also, but who live in a yard full of geldings?

How much freedom of movement do you give your horse?

How far would he travel if he was wild? Studies of some wild mustangs showed that they regularly walk up to 30 kilometers a day, depending on the availability of food.

> The Five Freedoms are very relevant when we look at the average horse in this country today. I think you'll agree that the horse in Europe generally enjoys many of the things associated with the first three Freedoms on the list, but most of us probably have some way to go in trying to meet those last two Freedoms.

PRIORITY BEHAVIOURS

Here is what behavioural scientists have identified as the most important behavioural needs in the horse and, also, how horses have prioritised them:

Order of Behavioural Priority. Which needs in the horse are being met by acting out these behaviours?

1.Reaction and response
■ Alarm raising through snorting, head raising, tail lifting, muscle tension
■ Self-defence

2.Grazing and drinking
■ Intake of food in phases
■ Basic health and survival

4.Rest and sleep
■ Idling, drowsing and sleeping
■ Body restoration and physical conservation – relaxation and rest standing up or lying down

3.Body care
■ Grooming
■ Stretching and rolling
■ Evacuation (urination and defecation)
■ Skin health
■ Physical care
■ Body hygiene

5.Motion
■ Running and playing
■ Exercise movements
■ Physical maintenance
■ Certain movements (like cantering) require regular expression to satisfy healthy horses

6.Exploration
- Investigative activities such as sheltering and ranging.
- Acquiring useful awareness and attentiveness to environment. Stimulation (varied and in quantity) that is satisfying and important for wellbeing

7.Territorialism
- Using individual space and that of whole herd – having a home base
- Spatial needs for nutrition, defence and shelter

8.Association
- Pair-bonding, playing
- Secure membership of the herd and safety to interact with others

An interesting environment at the Natural Animal Centre aids in the horses' puzzle-solving abilities.

Horses in harmony

One of the ways of looking at equine needs is to study the way a behavioural scientist might evaluate these. They tend to concentrate on working out how successful the horse is in terms of its integration with its environment. They would say that when most of the horse's needs are being met, it should function in a manner that is in harmony with its environment. So where do scientists start when they try to work out which behaviours or needs are more important than others to animals? Regardless of

the species being studied, they always try to start with the animal's maintenance behaviours – the survival behaviours that are critical to life. So in horses you might think these would be eating and drinking. But behavioural studies show that it is a lot more complicated than that, and we need to understand that needs go way beyond basic survival for life.

Understanding the table

The behaviours are shown in order of priority of needs. This means that a horse would not take

listed on the table. So equine scientists have learnt that the need to react and feel safe from threatening things takes over-riding priority in the horse.

Let's try to understand this by thinking about a horse that goes to a competition at the weekend. Because his safety needs are not being met – he is in a new environment that he perceives as threatening – he will not eat or drink the entire time he is away from his yard. Some of you may know horses that will even deny themselves the behaviours that are third and fourth on the table as well – they will not stale until they get back home and they certainly cannot rest or sleep because they feel the need to remain vigilant all the time.

At the Natural Animal Centre, we continually invest effort and time to ensure that the needs of our horses are met as often as is reasonably possible – and here's how:

1. Reaction and response – by being part of a stable, bonded herd, the needs of safety are met 24 hours a day as the herd is allowed to remain as a permanent group. A horse which is separated from the herd will remain fixedly staring at the herd in a state of vigilance until he is allowed to join the group. He cannot perform any other behaviours because this basic need has not been met.

2. Grazing and drinking – unless a horse feels safe within his group, he will not drink alongside another at a trough. This is why some horses never drink in the field, and only from their buckets in the stable at night. Being thirsty during the day, however, has a knock-on effect on the other needs being met – a horse will not play for example, if it is thirsty.

3. Body care – at the Natural Animal Centre, the horses have a large paddock in the summer which has dozens of enormous old oak trees under which they seek shade during the hottest time of the day – regulating temperature is an important need in physical well-being. They can also use the trees to self-groom which can be a difficult need to fulfil if the horse is stabled for long periods.

4. Rest and sleep – horses can only sleep if they feel safe enough to do so.

5. Motion – cantering and galloping are important expressions of kinetic needs in the horse.

6. Exploration – at the Natural Animal Centre, the horses have interesting environments to

care of his eating and drinking needs for example (number 2 on the table) unless he had first taken care of his reactivity needs (number 1 on the table). Similarly, he would not show a need to explore (number 6 on the table) unless all the other behavioural needs (1 to 5 on the table) had been met first.

So what is this all-important behaviour so strangely-termed 'reactivity'? A more commonplace word for reactivity is 'safety' which means that, unless a horse feels safe, he is unable to perform any of the other behaviours explore, including man-made mounds and ancient woodlands – this aids in puzzle-solving ability in the horses and ultimately helps make them easier to train.

7. Territorialism – individual space is important to the horse but permanent herds will often reduce their need for large individual space.

8. Association – social interaction is crucial for wellbeing in the horse. At the Natural Animal Centre, the horses are so well integrated that even horses that are not specifically pair-bonded to each other will freely interact.

CHAPTER FOUR

CLOSE TO NATURE

After reading this chapter, you should be able to answer questions on the following:

- What an ethologist does
- What an ethogram is
- Why understanding the horse ethogram is key to appreciating that a stable is nothing more than a cage
- How the Natural Animal Centre Winter Barn System works
- Why it works
- How to enrich the environment of the stabled horse
- How to enrich the life of the laminitic horse

Years ago, I remember sitting in a university lecture theatre watching videos of large numbers of dairy cows coming in from their field and going into the barn to be milked. Each cow knew and remembered which stall was hers and so there was very little charging and knocking about of each other. I thought that if a cow knew how to find her stall, horses too could find their own stables (without being led and without injury) when coming in from the field.

In the spring of 1997, my husband Ross and I set up the Natural Animal Centre with one very clear goal: to allow as many domesticated animals – from cats and dogs, to pigs, rabbits, chickens and horses – to live as natural a life as possible. I had never forgotten those videos of the loose cows and I was keen to see if we

Horses live in harmony with sheep and pigs at the Natural Animal Centre

could transport some of the cattle husbandry practices into looking after horses. Not that I wanted to turn horses into cattle, but I did want horses to have some of the responsibilities and choices that even the lowly cow had.

A permanent herd

We started by trying to find a mix of breeds of horses. I did not want a Thoroughbred herd or a Dartmoor pony herd for example – it was important that we could show people that all horses are the same when it comes to emotions and behavioural needs, no matter what breed they are. So we gradually acquired horses from rescue centres and we ended up with a mix of Thoroughbreds, Thoroughbred-draft crosses, a Dutch and British Warmblood, a Quarter Horse,

Horses and ponies of all shapes and sizes make up the Natural Animal Centre herd.

DOUBLE STANDARDS

We live in a culture where it is readily acceptable to sell horses that we no longer want (statistics show that the average horse in this country has six or seven homes in its lifetime, and the average pony has something more like 14!), yet most of us would never treat our cats or dogs in this way. We seem to have double standards when it comes to our mind-set towards certain animals and the horse is at the receiving end of the most complex and contradictory attitudes one could imagine.

I think it is fair to say that most books on horse care focus on the physical and nutritional care of the horse, but devote hardly any space to their emotional wellbeing. Such all-pervasive educational bias means that most of our horse yards across the country are all run along uniform lines (yard routines, feeding routines etc), with very few people questioning whether these practices constitute good psychological welfare for the horse.

However, by allowing the horses at the Natural Animal Centre to create a herd life 24 hours a day, 365 days a year, we hoped we would be able to show that even domesticated horses still have many of the same behaviours of their wild cousins, and by extension therefore, that maybe, at the NAC, many of their emotional and psychological needs were being met all or most of the time.

a Cleveland Bay, a Lipizzaner and a couple of native coloured cobs – a perfect mix.

In the early years of the Natural Animal Centre, we used to allow our working students to bring their own horses to the Centre and mix them in with our own herd, but this caused complications when people left and so, in more recent years, we have not had new horses join the herd. This has paid dividends in terms of the stability and sense of permanency in the

core Natural Animal Centre herd.

Now, we have a mix of six geldings and four mares but no stallions. Obviously, by not allowing the horses to breed has an impact on life in a herd but for a number of reasons, we have decided not to introduce stallions yet (although we will be rectifying this situation at a later stage). However, when the two cobs first arrived, they were both barely six months old (both having lost their mothers) and so we had

some compensation here in the balance of the herd, with the two youngsters needing a lot of nannying and nurturing from the older horses.

Natural life

Nearly all of the horses had come from poor backgrounds of abuse or neglect so that they too had to re-learn how to be horses again. Some of them had come to us labelled as untrainable or unridable, and I am firmly convinced that by allowing them to lead a more natural herd life we were more easily able to get them to a position where they accepted training again. It was (and still is!) so exciting to see the herd gel as a group, pair-bonds emerge, and watch horses grazing 16+ hours a day – all behaviours to be expected in the ethogram of the wild horse.

During summertime, the NAC herd enjoys 24-hours-a-day turnout in a large paddock which is surrounded with natural shelter from trees and shrubs. Woodland, man-made dips and mounds (as opposed to crushingly boring flat paddocks) make the environment more stimulating. Overall, we now see natural rhythms occurring in the life of the herd, such as moving across the field to drink as a group – the sort of thing you would see happening in the wild (wild horses are too much at risk from predation to drink on their own; the old safety-in-numbers adage still prevails), or moving into shade under the tall oaks to doze as a group.

In the wintertime, however, by allowing them to be in the field for most of the day, then come into the barns for shelter – pretty much just the same way most farmers keep their cows – we have managed to retain herd cohesion without affecting the horses' health and needs to keep warm and protected from wind and rain in the worst of the winter months.

The Natural Animal Centre Winter Barn System – how it works and why

This is how the ethogram works for the horses in the barns during winter at the NAC, with a comparison with the average life of most other domestic horses in Britain and their wild counterparts. You will see that, although the barn system is by no means perfect, it still goes a long way to meeting many of the important needs of the horses.

Horses in 'average' livery yards

- Live alone in a 'cage' for over 20 hours per day, on average.
- Limited turnout, anything from a 30 minute run in a school to about four or five hours per day in a field. Many yards practise no turnout at all during the winter or on rainy days.
- Turned out alone or in separate, single sex groups of mares or geldings only.
- Turned out in constantly changing groups as horses arrive or leave the yard. If a horse

does form a pair-bond, he is separated from his special friend when stabled for the bulk of the 24 hours.

- Fed manufactured concentrates from a bowl; hay fed in nets equivalent to one to four hour's grazing (ie from five to 25 per cent of natural grazing behaviours). No ability to move whilst eating.
- No access to leaves and bark in stable or school turnout.
- No choice as to whether horse would prefer to eat outside or inside when stabled.
- Abnormal sleep patterns because of over-long stabling and need to be 'on guard' all the time because stabled solitarily.

At the Natural Animal Centre, the barn system houses more than one species!

- Limited ability to act out normal play behaviours, either because stabled solitarily for most of day, or not turned out with same companions every day.

NAC horses – a way of letting horses achieve as much of the 'ideal' as possible

- Live in a permanent social group of 10.
- Permanent access to fields, tracks, outdoor arena and large barns 24-hours-a-day.
- Geldings and mares (and pigs and sheep!) permanently living together.
- Pair-bonds permanently living together.

- Pair-bonds eat, sleep and play together.
- 24-hour-a-day access to grass or hay. Crucially, horses like to walk-and-eat and this system allows them to fulfil this need.
- Hay supplemented with logs and twigs every day.
- 24-hour choice as to whether horse prefers to eat inside or outside barn.
- Sleeping patterns closer to natural because of more normal movement and eating, as well as permanent presence of other horses to 'stand guard'.
- 24-hour access to pair-bond (usually favourite play friend) as well as other herd members.

Wild Horses – the ultimate natural equine ethogram

- Live in permanent large social groups of (usually) up to 30 individuals.
- Continuous freedom to explore home range, to seek out shelter or open plains.
- Stallions and mares permanently living together, although at certain times of the year bachelor stallions form groups on the periphery of the main nursery herd of the mares, foals and dominant breeding stallion.
- Pair-bonds permanently living together.
- 24-hour-a-day access to grass and the ability to move at will (in the wild, horses have been known to frequently travel up to 30 kilometres per day – the distance they travel depends largely on availability of food).
- 24-hour-a-day access to browsing on trees and leaves (in certain parts of the world, this is reduced in extreme weather conditions of desert or snow).
- Able to find natural shelter.
- Normal sleeping patterns.
- Normal play behaviours because of being part of permanent social group.

My horse is still stabled. Can I improve his emotional wellbeing, even in this environment?

There are several things you can do!

1. If your horse has a pair-bond, make sure he is stabled next to his special friend. Even if they cannot touch each other, at least they can see each other close by. If the horses are in stalls,

Stabling pair-bonded horses together can improve emotional wellbeing.

they may even be able to groom and nuzzle each other throughout the night.

2. Tape off an area around the stable and occasionally feed your horse outside his stable. Better still, scatter his feed on the ground within the taped area as this will encourage foraging behaviours.

3. Similarly, spread the hay around the edges of the stable to encourage move-and-eat behaviours.

4. Give your horse branches and twigs to nibble and browse on. Many books will tell you which trees (such as yew) are toxic to horses and therefore need to be avoided.

These may all sound like very small things but compared to standing in an empty box/cage for hours on end, they considerably extend the choices of what to do for your horse.

My horse suffers from laminitis. I'd love to be able to turn him out but my vet says I must limit his grass intake. As a result I am forced to keep him in his stable. Is there another way?

Look at the Equine Ethogram Table – many of the behaviours shown do not revolve around eating. I have given advice to many rescue centres and, provided the vet pronounces the laminitic horse pain-free and fit for movement, then we can create areas where all those suffering from laminitis still have their other needs met. They are allowed to pair-bond, they are turned out all day into schools or areas where there is no grass, just stubble. They can still play and groom each other, in fact, have a pretty normal social life. In this way, their sleeping patterns are improved and they are less likely to become either depressed or aggressive. Just because a laminitic horse is unable to eat normally, it does not mean that we automatically have to take away the rest of his behaviours, also!

What does an ethologist do?

An ethologist is a person who studies the behaviour of animals in the wild. For example, I am currently spending a few months a year studying the behaviour of zebras in their wild environment in southern Africa. If, however, I

WHAT IS AN ETHOGRAM?

An ethogram is a list of behaviours drawn up by an ethologist when he studies a particular species of animal in the wild. Every species has its own repertoire of normal behaviours. Part of the horse ethogram, therefore, would be things like living in a herd, walking, eating, sleeping, playing etc. Only by knowing first what is the normal ethogram for the horse, can we, like equine ethologists, be in a position to judge what is abnormal behaviour in the horse.

tried to study zebras by studying the behaviour of a solitary specimen living in a zoo, I could not call myself an ethologist – knowing how the whole herd functions and behaves in a natural environment is crucial to an ethologist's understanding of that species.

If we truly want to understand more about how or why our own horse behaves in the way he does, we cannot make accurate interpretations about his behaviour if the horse is never turned out with mares, for example, or if he spends most of his day alone in a 12' by 12' stable.

Food for thought – does your horse live in a stable or a cage?

DO WE CAGE HORSES?

A couple of years ago, we ran a campaign where we asked horses owners to not use the word 'stable' for a period of one week and instead, substitute the word 'cage'. People were asked to say, "I am just going to pop my horse back into his cage," or to ring the yard staff from work and say, "I have to work late tonight and won't be able to ride – just leave my horse in his cage until tomorrow morning." The campaign was overwhelmingly successful and literally hundreds of people rang to say that they had not realised that just because we all use the euphemism 'stable', it does not excuse the fact that a 12' by 12' box is nothing more than a cage from the horse's point of view. Add to the fact that most horses in Britain and Europe spend around 21 or 22 hours per day in their 'cage' and then overlay this with knowledge on how horses behave according to their natural ethogram, it is not too difficult to realise there is a fairly major conflict occurring between the way we habitually keep horses and the way they would behave, if given more freedom.

I think that deep down inside all of us (even without formal scientific training), we all know that the horse wants to behave like a horse, but it is so hard to hold onto that concept when all the horses around you are enduring such unnatural management practices. So although I too firmly believed that because the horse is a horse, it will behave like a horse, it was by bringing together a permanent herd at the Natural Animal Centre that I finally saw domestic horses revealing their natural side – their normal ethogram if you like – bit by bit.

CHAPTER FIVE

SAFETY IN NUMBERS

After reading this chapter, you should be able to answer questions on the following:
- How to prepare horses for conversion to the Barn System, first in a field then in a barn
- How to keep the System running peacefully and safely
- The need for social stability in the System
- How to introduce the under-socialised horse to the System
- How to deal with a food-aggressive horse

One of the most frequently asked questions by people who see our herd of horses wandering around in the barn is that it must be impossible to feed all 10 horses loose in the barn at once. And the simple answer to that is 'No' – it is really easy. Just as I said in a previous chapter, if a cow can learn to find its way to its own stall to be milked, then surely a horse can be taught to go to its own place for feeding, too?

Originally, when the horses came to the Centre, they were all on different kinds of short feed and were fed different quantities – much like you would find in any livery yard. This is how we taught the horses relatively quickly to remain with their buckets and not to steal their neighbours' food.

Field practice

We started off by practising with the horses in the summer in an open field. Horses were allowed to eat with the buckets spaced far apart so that, if there was any chasing from bowls,

there was no danger of a horse getting injured. As the horses started to understand what was required of them – that is, 'remain at your own bucket' – we taped them into a smaller and smaller area, until eventually they were eating quietly in a space the size equivalent to the barn they would be transferred into in the winter.

Whilst out in the field, we placed large piles of hay next to each horse's bucket – there are always horses that are faster eaters than others, and we wanted to be sure that these 'gobblers' did not automatically turn to steal the next horse's food when they had finished theirs. We achieved this largely by giving them plenty of hay – right at their buckets. Most of the horses just finished their food and immediately tucked into their hay.

Introducing the Barn System

Once we believed that the horses had had enough practice in the field, we transferred them to the barn, only putting out hay at first. They were relatively used to being loose within a certain sized space because of the field practice but the barn was in a different area, had a roof on it and is, of course, darker than the open field. All these factors can affect the horses and it was important that we were not over-confident and allowed the horses a period of time for adjusting to their new surroundings. By giving them hay only when they first arrived, we achieved a smooth transition from field to barn without any disruption.

In just the same way as we did before, we had to teach each horse where its own place or station was for feeding. We arranged the horses in an order of placing which was identical to what they had become used to in the field. They quickly settled into their new surroundings and, when short feed was introduced, we again made sure that there was plenty of hay for each horse next to the feed bucket. Once every horse had finished feeding we removed all the buckets and the horses learnt that this was the cue that it was now OK to move freely around the barn.

No threats

We made sure that things continued to run peacefully by always ensuring there were more hay piles scattered around the barn than there were horses. In this way, no rows could break out over hay. One of the most important safety features that we have incorporated into the barn is something we jokingly refer to at the Centre

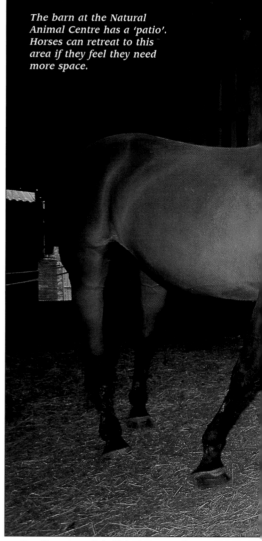

The barn at the Natural Animal Centre has a 'patio'. Horses can retreat to this area if they feel they need more space.

as the 'horse patio'. This is a small concrete yard just outside the barn doors. If ever a horse feels threatened by another (and over the last couple of winters, as the permanency of the herd has become entrenched, these incidents have dwindled to hardly any number at all), it always had the choice and opportunity to 'escape' out of the barn onto the horse patio.

During those first few weeks, the patio was an invaluable place of refuge for some of the horses who were adjusting at a slower rate than others. Nowadays, we still have a situation where one or two of the herd has remained keen to eat outside the barn on the 'patio' and we are happy to accommodate this preference.

Close to nature

The horse is a species that prefers to eat on the move. Watch any horse in a field and you will see that they rarely remain in one place – they graze-and-move, graze-and-move. This is one of the chief reasons we went to all the efforts described above to get the Centre's horses settled in the barn. By scattering lots of hay around the barn (unlimited, from the horses' perspective), we had got as close as we possibly could to meeting a crucial natural need of the horses eating on the move all night long.

Even in winter, we meet their natural browsing needs (horses will take up to 10 per cent of their diet in the form of branches, bark

and leaves) by placing logs in the barn for them to strip for bark and, whenever possible, we give them branches to nibble on.

In the late winter, when availability of branches and leaves becomes scarce, we place vegetables and fruit, such as carrots, parsnips and apples, in the bed of the barn. By hiding these tasty delicacies, we encourage foraging and exploratory behaviours in the horses – and the horses did not take long to learn that these 'treasure hunts' yielded pleasurable rewards.

The barn system allows pair-bonds to be together and to forage for carrots and other delicacies hidden in the straw.

How does the Barn System work in terms of social hierarchies – do the horses fight because they can move freely?

In Chapter Two, I explained that behavioural scientists have learnt that social animals have a structure or set of 'rules' which enables all the animals in the group to get along with minimal upsurges of aggression. Part of that structure includes being able to recognise at which point it is better to submit or defer to another animal which is probably more dominant. For a social structure to work smoothly in a group of animals in the wild, three key things are crucial:

■ Animals must be able to recognise each member of the group.

■ Animals need to have a long-term memory

ARE TOYS THE ANSWER?

Whilst I am in no way against stable toys that one can purchase, I do question owners who rely on one solitary ball hanging from the ceiling as being enough in terms of diversion or environmental enrichment for a horse that is stabled for 18 or 20 hours per day. Playing 'treasure hunts' with your horse – even if you just do this in the stable – will be a much more rewarding pastime for your horse, and possibly a lot less frustrating!

that is more akin to a herd in the wild. Without this stability, it would be extremely difficult to keep horses loose in an open barn.

But it is this very sense of permanency that is so often lacking in the average horse today. We buy and sell them as though they were motor cars; we move them from yard to yard to suit our convenience or pocket, and many yards do not operate turnout regimes which allow for the building of long-term equine bonds. Yet making these life-long attachments is a very important need in the natural horse and by ignoring these desires, we compromise our horses' emotional welfare.

Sometimes, when I am helping owners convert their horses to the Barn System, I come across some horses that initially have socialisation problems with other horses. Wherever possible, I always try to ensure that an under-socialised horse is not isolated from the others. Typically, I would set up a system where we tape off an area within the barn until the horse is acclimatised to horses around him.

Under-socialised horses are often frightened of being approached, even though they present their emotions in the form of fear-aggressive behaviour. This is because they have become sensitised to their own personal space and when that is breached, they over-react. By allowing them to eat hay alongside the others, but without fear of having their space invaded, you will allow the horse to gradually work out that there is no need to lunge out at the others. As he improves, increase the size of the taped-off area and add another horse. Eventually, you will be able to release the pair into the whole herd without any further aggressive behaviour from the horse.

which they can rely on to remember the outcome of previous encounters with other animals in the group.
- The group needs to be relatively stable and permanent (occasional deaths from predators or natural causes aside).

By bringing a herd together at the Centre, and by not constantly adding horses or selling others off, we have achieved the kind of permanency

Help your horses get used to the idea of having other horses around at feed and watering times by practising in a field first.

Dealing with food-aggressive horses

Although it may be interesting to read about the Winter Barn System, you may be stuck with keeping your horse in a stable at the moment – and what if he behaves aggressively at feeding time? Is there anything you can take from the Barn System that could help him?

When I am asked to help with a food aggressive horse, the type that nips his owner if she enters his stable when he is eating, or the one that will charge anyone in the immediate radius when he has a bowl of food, one of the most reliable ways of improving the behaviour is to allow the horse to move while it is eating. Tape off an area in front of your horse's stable or, if there is a small yard available, even better. Scatter your horse's feed all around the area on the ground so that he can move around as he eats. It is not just the moving that helps (because it allows the horse to eat in a natural way) but it is also the fact that he does not have a stationary bucket to guard or protect.

Strange as it may at first seem, aggression at feeding time is a fear-based behaviour. Horses that have been starved previously are often the worst in terms of food-related aggression. It is the fear of not having enough to eat, or historically, from the horse's point of view, having been proved right that he did not always have enough to eat, that causes the fear-aggression. In this sense, the horse believes that he is behaving quite rationally!

I am not saying that all food-aggressive horses have been starved, but it may mean that the horse is not receiving enough opportunity to act out natural grazing behaviours. Being fed from a bucket, or made to eat hay standing still because it is presented in a haynet, can cause aggressive behaviour.

Remember that in the wild an average horse would graze around 16 hours a day. By encouraging natural foraging behaviours by scatter feeding, and then supplementing this with a number of piles of hay which he can move around to, can pay enormous dividends in easing your horse's food-related anxieties.

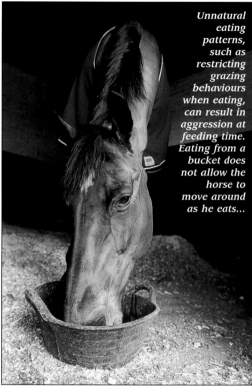

Unnatural eating patterns, such as restricting grazing behaviours when eating, can result in aggression at feeding time. Eating from a bucket does not allow the horse to move around as he eats...

... and eating from a haynet also restricts the horse in the same way.

KEEPING THE PEACE

After reading this chapter, you should be able to answer questions on the following:

- The equine social system of followership
- How the alpha mare attains her alpha status
- Why training systems based on human dominance of the horse are misplaced from the horse's perspective
- The aggression-submission continuum
- The subtlety of horse emotional communication
- Types of aggression

Horses are not naturally aggressive – for good survival reasons – and in the wild, herds tend to follow an alpha mare, rather than a dominant male. So isn't it unnecessarily aggressive of us to try to dominate our own horses when we train them? To answer this question, we need to explore a little more why horses choose to live in groups in the first place.

The vast majority of species of animals on this planet opt to live in groups rather than follow a solitary existence. But making hasty assumptions that all of them choose group living just because they want to be among friends is not always appropriate. Take the honeybee, for example. Being part of a group in this case involves subjugation of individuality as the bees

Horses live in groups because the benefits of doing so outweigh a solitary existence.

toil away their lives for the greater good of the whole hive. Behavioural scientists believe that for many species of penguin being part of a group is motivated primarily by pure survival needs for physical warmth, as penguins take it in turns to be on the outside of a circle and shield the other members from the brunt of their polar environment.

It is generally accepted that many prey animal species, including horses, live in groups because the benefits of doing so outweigh a solitary existence. Having other members around you to share in keeping a lookout for danger is an obvious benefit, as well as having easy access to someone to mate with, play with or groom you. Group living is not without its downsides, however. Being part of a group means that you are more conspicuous, and it therefore increases the risk of being easily spotted by predators, compared to being able to hide secretively as a solitary individual. Being part of a herd also increases the horse's chances of succumbing to disease or injury as a result of horse-on-horse interactions.

Herd harmony

Ask an equine behavioural scientist to single out the most striking and persistent behaviour in horses and it is unlikely that you would get a unanimous response. It is not unreasonable to

When the alpha mare decides it is the right, safe time for the herd to more to a drinking hole, she simply leaves – and the rest of the herd follows.

suggest that most of them would agree that the highly co-operative, affiliative behaviour between members of the same herd is a very common trait. When considering the nature of equine aggression, it is important to understand from the outset that this is a rather strange question because horses are not, by nature, an overtly aggressive species. Rather than risk instability and injury through persistent aggressive encounters, most horses ensure that other herd members understand that resolving differences by avoiding a fight is a key strategy.

Of course, there are always instances where a horse might decide to resort to aggression when threatened by another herd member over something that is too important to simply ignore. A mare whose young foal is threatened by another horse will not typically turn the other cheek, but will defend her youngster in a display known as maternal aggression. But outside of these types of situations, keeping harmony and cohesiveness in the herd by sorting out differences without disruption is the name of the game as far as the horse is concerned. At the very least, as a prey animal, the horse cannot afford to make himself vulnerable to predators by risking injury in too many contests, and I described in Chapter Two how important the decision to submit can be in resolving hierarchy disputes in the herd.

Follow me!

For decades, scientists studying cattle behaviour were aware of the concept of followership amongst cows. More recently, equine behaviourists have agreed that a similar principle of leadership occurs in horses also. The myth that a strong, virile stallion was herd leader was exploded as behaviourists learnt that horses in the wild are typically led by an alpha female. But unless you appreciate the fundamental philosophy in the horse – that aggressive dominance displays are to be mainly avoided – how she demonstrates her leadership may seem a little strange.

When the mare decides it is the right, safe time for the herd to move to a drinking hole, she simply leaves – and the rest of the herd follows. She does not run around asserting her leadership by coercing the other horses to comply; it is a passive demonstration of unequivocal, uncontested alpha status. Why the others agree to follow her is now thought to depend on a number of factors which include:

■ **Whose genes the mare has inherited.** Alpha mares are often daughters or grand-daughters of previous herd leaders, so inheriting your mother's leadership genes seems to be important.

■ **The age of the mare and how long she has been resident in the herd.** Young mares, or those which have recently joined a herd, do not rise immediately to leader status. The longer the mare has been in a herd, the more likely she is to reach the position where the others agree to follow her.

■ **Experience.** Knowing where to lead the herd to so that the best grazing, the best shelter and so on, can be found is essential. Inexperienced mares might lead the herd into unsuitable territories, thereby placing the whole herd at risk from starvation, thirst or other dangers. By contrast, experienced alpha mares can lead the herd to favourite seasonal grazing areas, and even to seldom-visited places that perhaps only they experienced when their mothers were leaders.

FOLLOWERSHIP – NOT DOMINANCE!

Whilst the followership principle in horse behaviour is known in scientific circles, to date, unfortunately, the information has not been easily accessible to most horse owners. Books and videos for horse lovers abound with advice for controlling the horse based on phrases such as, "Show the horse who is boss," and, "learn to be the alpha horse," or make the horse show you "respect". Such commonplace parlance in horse training has no basis in scientific equine behavioural analysis, however. This is why having a knowledge of horse behaviour is both helpful and important in the management and training of your horse.

If you would like to learn more about training your horse using the natural equine principle of followership, follow the Positive Horse Magic Distance Learning programme devised by Ross and Heather Simpson. (See Part Three for more on this.)

TYPES OF AGGRESSION

Behavioural scientists have long recognised that to suggest that an animal is 'aggressive' is an incomplete label that does not take into account the motivation for the display. But before we look at some of the different types of aggression which have been identified in horses, it is worth pausing to note that aggressive behaviour is not uniform or absolute in its intensity of expression. What I mean by this, is that aggressive behaviours are part of an aggression-submission continuum.

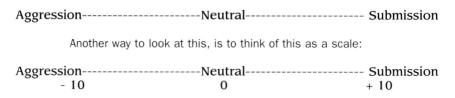

Aggression----------------------Neutral---------------------- Submission

Another way to look at this, is to think of this as a scale:

Aggression----------------------Neutral---------------------- Submission
   - 10   0   + 10

Between neutral (or zero) and full-blown aggression (-10), there are a number of phases of aggression. In wolves, and to some extent dogs, these phases of aggression have been identified (there are almost 30 phases) where just a stare might be seen as Phase One on the aggressive side of the scale, and a bite-plus-pinning-down could be the ultimate display of aggression. By the same token, wolf ethologists have identified around 10 phases of submission, from a slight aversion of eye contact, to submissive urination as the wolf displays its belly.

Read the signs

The detail of the phases of aggression and submission in horses has not yet been scientifically researched in full detail, but that these phases exist is in no doubt. The important thing for you to know at this stage, however, is that by the time people typically become aware of aggression towards them by a healthy horse (such as the horse biting them, or lashing out offensively and kicking them with his foreleg), the initial, subtle phases of aggression will have been displayed, but probably gone unnoticed by the owner.

The primary strategy for the horse using phases in aggression displays is to avoid a fight and injury. In every combative encounter, two horses can therefore communicate to each other that they are still in a position to escalate aggression unless the other backs down. Alternatively, if they believe they are going to lose the contest, they might start by showing low, milder phases of submission – but if they remain under threat, they would continue to move through the phases to more extreme submission.

Why might horses be aggressive?

It is extremely rare for a healthy, psychologically well-adjusted horse to show a high phase of aggression towards a person without going through the phases, and claims that, "the horse lashed out with no warning," or, "bit me for no reason," are highly unlikely. Learning to read your horse's body language is like learning to speak a foreign language – it takes patience and diligence, but the communication signals are there for us to behold.

Facial expressions

In an amazing coincidence the horse, like the wolf, appears to use a number of facial features, such as eye contact, in communication between individuals in the group. Lip positions and eyebrow movements are now recognised by behavioural scientists as being reflections of the horse's emotional state with respect to aggression or submission. A cock of your horse's eyebrow is a long way off from him biting your arm, so understanding the subtle behaviours that change by degrees is an important step in appreciating the nature of equine aggression.

Horses appear to use a number of facial features, such as eye contact, in communication with others in the herd.

Behaviourists have identified a number of different types of aggression. Here are some:

Type of Aggression and Example of Motivation for Display

1. Dominance: Horse drives another away from access to shadiest part under a tree.

2. Fear: Horse kicks farrier as he is frightened of being shod.

3. Territorial: Horse threatens to kick owner when she enters stable (fear-based behaviour).

4. Maternal: Mare chases man away from her foal as she is fearful of people.

5. Sexual: A stallion drives other stallions away from his harem of mares to ensure he is the only horse that reproduces with them.

6. Pain: A horse lashes at a vet with his foreleg during a painful examination.

7. Redirected: A frustrated horse tied up tight and short to a wall is unable to show aggression to a person standing near his head so kicks out at a passing horse instead.

8. Food: Horse kicks out at other horses if they pass too close behind him whilst he is eating from his bowl (this is a fear-based behaviour).

9. Learned: Horse learns that lungeing at his owner with his teeth stops her tightening his girth too quickly.

10. Idiopathic: A term that means that the cause of the aggression is unknown; for example, a vet finds nothing physically wrong that might cause pain-induced aggression, and a behavioural scientist cannot identify the motivation, either. This behaviour might stem from genetic factors that would be difficult to quantify, for example, a particular breeding line might have a record of aggressive horses.

This table is, of course, necessarily simplified and the motivations for aggression can often be extremely complex and varied. It is also not uncommon to find aggression being motivated by more than one cause.

Showing fear or pain aggression when being saddled is a learned behaviour.

CHAPTER SEVEN

ADAPTION PROBLEMS

After reading this chapter, you should be able to answer questions on the following:

- Why outbreaks in domestic horse aggression are problems of adaption
- How territorial behaviour can arise in the horse
- Why territorial behaviour is motivated by fear
- Causes of food-related aggression in the horse
- Why training strategies based on the human as 'alpha' are inappropriate for the horse

I n the previous chapter, I explained that horses usually go out of their way to avoid aggressive encounters with other horses as much as possible. So why do we often see aggression directed at other horses and, sometimes, even ourselves? Successful evolutionary strategies that have been tried and tested over millions and millions of years play a major part in governing how our horses behave today. But the horse's association with man has been extremely short, relatively-speaking (a few thousand years, rather than millions) and, in more recent times, restrictive management regimes of horses have become a far cry from the free-ranging lifestyle of the horse's ancestors.

Most equine behavioural scientists agree that the vast majority of outbreaks of aggression in yards, either between horses or directed at ourselves, is a direct result of the horse's struggle to adapt to modern circumstances. To illustrate the point, I will look at two common types of aggression in the domestic horse – territorial aggression, and food-related aggression.

Territorial aggression

Studies of wild herds of horses on several continents have shown that, although a herd may often have a preference for certain areas for grazing, shelter and drinking (the home range), these areas can often overlap with the home ranges of other herds. When grazing, shelter and water is in plentiful supply, wild horses show little tendency to drive away strange herds. In places like Newfoundland, Canada, where ponies have, to all intents and purposes, unlimited space, a number of herds have still been observed grazing peaceably together wherever their home ranges overlap. But when any one of these resources becomes scarce – say, grazing is limited because of adverse weather conditions – then the herd

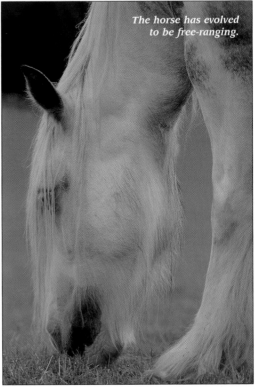

The horse has evolved to be free-ranging.

becomes territorial over their range and will defend their area from invasion by another herd. The scarcity of the resource (in this case, of potentially life-giving importance) causes the herd to transform from a tolerant entity into one that will resort to territorial aggression where necessary, to preserve a selfish and constant access to their food supply.

A herd does not show aggression to the second herd by fighting them in close combat (such as we might see in human, warlike behaviours) but simply drives the strange horses out, usually with no physical contact between the groups at all. Having the ability to assert an aggressive intention successfully without the use of physical coercion is an alien concept to us humans, but it is important for us to remember the equine strategy when we train and manage our horses. Just because a horse hasn't physically bitten or kicked, doesn't mean he's happy!

Space invaders

For the strategy of non-physical contact to work, one crucial thing needs to exist in the environment: space. In the wild, a fleeing herd has the space to escape territorial overtures from the other horses and everyone usually survives the encounter unharmed. In most modern yards however, domestic horses do not enjoy the luxury of space. If a new horse is suddenly added to an existing small group because his owner has recently hired a box at the yard, his position is akin to that of a wild horse in an invading herd in the situation described above. Grazing is certainly scarce from the perspective of the existing herd, and possibly shelter, too. The herd may, therefore, become territorially aggressive and attempt to drive the new arrival out of their home range. If there were no fences to stop their flight, the majority of domestic horses would be able to make their escape without resorting to a heightened phase of aggression such as I described in the previous chapter. But, sadly, there almost always will be fences blocking the path of the new horse. The only way he can demonstrate his desire to avoid escalating aggression from the established herd, is to exercise a simulated flight response by going round and round the paddock. Unfortunately, getting trapped in corners of the paddock is often an inevitable result and as soon as the new horse appears to exhibit a 'refusal' to flee,

A new horses often gets trapped in a corner of a paddock, and he has no choice but to react defensively with respect to his personal space.

Play behaviours in horses can easily be mistaken for aggression . . .

the existing herd resorts to fight behaviours, sometimes kicking or biting the hapless individual. The new horse's only chance to avoid physical aggression is to somehow extricate himself from the corner of the paddock and then resume the same oblong flight path along the fence line, or to try protecting himself by turning his rump on the others and defending his personal space by lashing out at anyone that gets too close.

Interestingly, often even the horses in the established herd will attack by kicking out with their hindlegs also, a clear indication that their so-called aggression is actually a defensive response to a need to protect their own space, both personal and that of the whole group. This is why behavioural scientists often equate territorial aggression to guarding behaviours that are fear-based – just think, you really only guard what you feel is worth fighting over and what you think you might lose. Even dogs like Rottweilers and German Shepherds have had their natural fear-based territorial behaviours manipulated for our benefit. They may be fearsome protectors of their owners' homes, but the principle of fear of being invaded is still the same – even for big, strong dogs.

Play fighting

As far as equine territorial displays are concerned, do not mistake play behaviours in horses for aggression. I often hear of a new horse being separated from his new equine friends because the owner has misinterpreted play between the group – actually a profound sign of acceptance of the new horse – as being fighting. The simple solution to avoid this happening is for you to learn more about horse play behaviours, either by doing some reading or attending a horse behaviour course.

. . . leading to a new horse being removed from the scene.

Some common questions raised about territorial aggression:

In an existing herd, is the horse that seems unable to accept a new horse likely to be the most dominant individual in the herd, particularly if he is the only one that tries to corner and kick the new arrival?

While, of course, every situation needs to be assessed individually, in general the horse that believes he has the most to lose might exhibit the highest level of fear aggression, and therefore could be motivated to take the most physical action. This behaviour is not a display of dominance, but rather of fear-induced territorial defence.

Is a horse that turns his rump on his owner when she tries to enter his stable displaying dominance towards her? Is this the time to show the horse you are his alpha and that he needs to show you respect?

Again, individual circumstances may apply but this is yet another example of a horse using the

threat of defensive aggression to defend an extremely scarce resource: his space, a mere 12' by 12' average stable area. Heavy-handed techniques, forcing the horse to submit, may sometimes appear to work but are, in fact, entirely misplaced because the horse's behaviour is nothing to do with dominance at all! These so-called 'dominance-reduction' approaches sometimes appear to work but in reality they will tend to make the horse bury his fear rather than lose it.

Behaviour modification techniques used by qualified equine behaviourists (such as those used by students that study the EBQ at the Natural Animal Centre) are geared towards building the horse's trust in the owner and teach him (through counter-conditioning and positive reinforcement of good behaviours) not to react to the presence of a human on his 'patch'.

Don't Steal my Food!

One of the most common types of horse aggression that I am asked to assist with in private consultancy is food-related aggression. A horse that is possessive about his bowl or his hay believes he has to display aggression to people or other horses because he thinks he

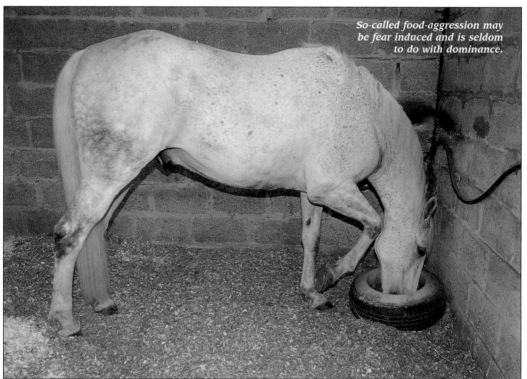

So-called food-aggression may be fear induced and is seldom to do with dominance.

may lose the food. Again, food-related aggression is almost always fear-induced and seldom anything to do with dominance.

A horse that threatens you every time you approach him whilst he is eating can be very upsetting. So why could he be behaving like this?

One reason could be abrupt, early weaning – taking the foal away from his mother much sooner than in nature. In studies of puppies that were abruptly weaned from their mother through human interference at less than six weeks of age (approximately 50 per cent younger than they would be if weaned naturally) and were all fed out of one bowl (forced to compete for food), mainly grew up to be food aggressive towards their human owners. Similar studies have not been performed on horses but it is not unreasonable to deduce that abrupt, early weaning is likely to play a role in the development of equine possessive aggression.

Speaking from experience

Previous bad experiences related to humans removing food may be a factor in food-related aggression in horses. Take Teddy, a 12-year-old Thoroughbred–cross that lives with our herd at the Natural Animal Centre. When he first came to the Natural Animal Centre, three years ago, one of the biggest issues we had to deal with was his food-related aggression. Because we manage the herd under the Barn System during winter nights, Teddy (who was, probably for the first time in his life, unconstrained by a stable) had a free rein in exhibiting the worst of his aggression. Not only would he lash out vigorously with his hind legs if any man, horse, dog or cat walked behind him whilst he was eating, he would also sometimes reverse really fast into any unsuspecting passer-by up to 20 feet away from him, then apply the same kicking strategy.

Prior to coming to the Natural Animal Centre, Teddy had had the misfortune in life to be starved twice. Losing such a vital resource not just once, but twice, caused him to become psychologically damaged in the sense that the experiences had scarred him so deeply that the merest sight of a human on the horizon when he had food was enough to spark off an intense aggressive response. Without behaviour modification assistance, a horse like Teddy

Abrupt, early weaning can be responsible for equine possesive aggression.

could react like this for the rest of his life. Fortunately, he responded well to a modification programme at the Natural Animal Centre, and quickly became safe to be around during feeding times.

And it is not just starving that causes problems. Horses which are chronically confined in stables are sometimes given too much to eat, whilst others are given too little. Both situations can also contribute to aggressive reactions in the horse so it is not always appropriate to jump to conclusions that previous bad experiences are to blame for food-related aggression. Generally speaking, however, food related aggression can be easily modified and the horse – like Teddy – can often show a complete recovery.

In summary, therefore, we should remember

In a free-ranging environment, wild horses exhibit strong, co-operative affiliative behaviours where heightened physical aggression has little place.

that horses, like many other social animals, rely on avoidance strategies to minimise aggressive encounters and it is usually only man-made management regimes and practices that cause equine aggression to come repeatedly to the fore. By contrast, in a free-ranging environment, wild horses exhibit strong co-operative, affiliative behaviours where heightened physical aggression has little place. Accordingly, we need to re-think our common recourse to dominance-oriented disciplinary methods in our interactions

with horses as they do not make sense to the horse, and are likely to increase his fear and suspicion of humans.

Just because the horse's natural behavioural response of followership may make the human think his 'dominance-reduction' strategies have caused the horse to comply, inevitably, in these circumstances, the horse has only submitted by suppressing his behaviours, rather than reaching a trusting agreement with the handler.

C H A P T E R   E I G H T

FIRST IMPRESSIONS ARE LASTING

After reading this chapter, you should be able to answer questions on the following:

- The difference between a precocial and altricial species
- The timetable of foal behavioural development
- Why humans should not interfere with this timetable
- Why so-called 'foal imprinting' training is inappropriate
- The first group activity in a foal's life
- Behavioural consequences on the foal of early separation from the mare

Our horses' early experiences in the vital early months of their lives shape their behaviour for years to come. It is for this reason that I will now spend some time looking at the behavioural development of the foal. Even if you do not own a young horse at present, or have no intention of ever breeding one, if you want to gain a greater insight into your adult horse's temperament and behaviour then you need an appreciation of how that behaviour has developed – from the first few seconds in life.

Baby horses, baby humans

Horses are a precocial species. This means that if you are a prey animal (as horses are) then it is a good evolutionary adaption to develop very quickly once you leave the womb, so that you are ready to run away from danger with the herd within an hour or two of being born.

Humans, on the other hand, are altricial. They develop very slowly as children, not walking until they about a year old – and then still have to rely on parental support and care until they are in their teens.

For horses, being precocial means that, from the moment of birth, the foal needs to develop at a pace which is nothing short of breathtaking. Think about what is going on inside the foal's body to get it from the point of lifting its neck in the first five minutes of life, to cantering about 90 minutes later. Ethologists have studied these early crucial minutes in a foal's life and there are a number of critical things that need to happen if the foal is to develop normally. If some or all of these do not occur, the horse could behave abnormally for the rest of his life.

The initial movements of the foal take place in a certain sequence and according to a specific time schedule (see the table below). For instance, once born, a foal should raise his head and neck and move so that he lies on his breastbone. Behavioural scientists believe that one of the reasons this happens so quickly is to allow the mare the opportunity to lick the foal all over his body. The ears should start to move so that the foal begins to orientate himself and then, after flexion of his legs, he is ready to make his first attempt at a wobbly stand. All this takes place in under 30 minutes.

Behaviour	Minutes after birth in which behaviour occurs
Lifts head	1 to 5
Rolls over onto sternum	5
Lifts and starts moving ears	5 to 10
First attempt at standing	5 to 10
Successful standing	25 to 50
First suckling	35 to 60
First walk	60 to 90
First trot	90 to 120

A precocial species, equine foals have evolved to develop quickly so they can run away from danger with the herd within an hour or two of their birth.

Within minutes of giving birth, the mare turns to sniff and lick her foal.

The mare and foal need to recognise each other

Horses tend to give birth at similar times and so it is vital that mother and baby can recognise each other from the rest of the group. Within minutes of the foal being born, the mare turns to sniff and lick her foal. The function of this behaviour serves to ensure that a mare will always recognize her foal by its scent and, of course, make sure that she does not suckle the wrong foal in the future. She also nickers to the foal and this cue, coupled with the tactile experience of being licked, helps the foal learn both what his mother smells and sounds like so that he too can recognize her, even from a very early age. It may seem strange to think that the foal relies on these cues when you would think that the most obvious cue would be a visual one but, in fact, foals are myopic (short-sighted) initially and their mothers must at first appear like a blur. This myopia also accounts for why foals so often to us appear clumsy, stumbling into objects.

Imprinting – facts and fallacies

There has been much talk about 'foal imprinting', with some horse trainers suggesting you can learn how to imprint your foal to yourself. From a scientific perspective, such practices lack substance because, technically, true imprinting is a form of rapid or instant learning at a critical phase and is an essential part of an animal learning what species it is, as well as who its mother is. In this sense, if you genuinely were to imprint a foal to yourself, you would end up with an animal that did not know it was a horse (and therefore would not know how to behave like a horse) and one that would look to you to be its mother. What many people understand erroneously to be 'foal imprinting' is, therefore, in fact merely attempts at habituation of the young foal to humans, as well as some early basic training.

The famous ethologist, Konrad Lorenz, showed that imprinting in its purest form is present in birds only, but that there are correlations in mammal species, also. Lorenz took goslings that had been incubated artificially and then imprinted them to himself as he was the first thing they set eyes on once they were hatched. Lorenz genuinely interrupted the goslings' learning of species identity as they all followed him as though he was their parent.

Another example of pure imprinting occurs in zebras when, just after giving birth, the mare holds her face directly in front of her foal's eyes for the first 30 minutes of life so that he can learn the pattern of her stripes, crucial for his ability to recognize her later amongst a herd of similarly striped animals.

So in many ways it is a good thing that horses do not easily imprint onto humans as this saves them from being interfered with too much from over-eager people – not least because a person would have to substitute themselves into the role of the mare and spend 12 hours a day alongside the foal!

The foal needs to orientate himself

People who observe newborn foals all marvel at the amount of exploring the youngster does. He touches the ground and objects around him, starting to gain a familiarity of his environment. Because the foal's vision is poor at this time, he noses his mother and she quickly becomes the prime focus of his attention.

For the first weeks of his life, the foal's time is divided between paying attention to his mother, suckling and grazing, and exploring.

Behavioural scientists believe it is the underbelly of the mare that provides a vital cue in the orientation of the foal: his starting point. Although it is not uncommon for a foal to try at first to suckle objects surrounding him, the mare never interferes with this crucial orientation process and will wait patiently for the foal to find her mammary region on his own. It is important that humans do not try to guide or force the foal to the mare's teats. The more humans interfere, the more likely things could go wrong – and a foal that is forced into certain movements could grow up frightened of people. Human interference can also cause rejection of the foal by the mare or maternal aggression in the mare, particularly if she has had past bad experiences with humans.

The foal needs to stretch his body – known as pandiculation. This will be examined further in the next chapter when we look at the development of play behaviour in horses. At this point remember that stretching behaviours are an important part of the development of physical well-being in the young foal.

A social debut

For the first several weeks of his life, the foal spends a large proportion of his time resting. His waking moments are divided between paying attention to his mother, suckling and grazing, and exploring. Very young foals are fearless and will wander from their mother's side but are quickly restored to their rightful position by the vigilant mare. Ethologists studying wild horses have noted that foals tend to rest in groups and this is the first group activity which a foal experiences. Gradually, the focus of the foal will begin to move away from an exclusive attention to the mare, to an increasing awareness of his peers. How he begins to interact with other foals is the subject of the next chapter.

Some common questions about foal behavioural development

What might the behavioural consequences be for a foal separated from its mother at birth?

The interaction between mare and foal immediately after the birth is crucial for the foal to grow up both physically and psychologically well-adjusted. In the 1950's, a psychologist, Harry Harlow, studied the effects of social deprivation in baby rhesus monkeys. He isolated them completely from their mothers and other monkeys and proved that when they were reintroduced to monkeys at a later stage, they were terrified of their peers. He also discovered that the deprived monkeys were unable to communicate effectively as they could neither read primate facial expressions, nor pass on messages with their own facial features.

Nowadays we would consider such experiments inhumane and cruel but some positive things did come out of the research in that we can use these results in our understanding of the behavioural development of many mammals, and certainly that of horses.

Do artificial weaning practices have an adverse effect on the future behaviour of the foal?

In the wild and left to her own devices, a mare will start to wean her foal just before she is due to foal again. If she is not in foal again, the current foal will not be weaned until the end of the second year (although, of course, the yearling would be suckling a lot less than a newborn one would). In Great Britain it is the practice of many breeders, both at large studs and those who would not consider themselves to be professional breeders, to artificially wean a foal from its mother during the period of four to six months after birth. But removing a foal abruptly from its mother and locking it in a stable does not happen in the wild.

Also, when a mare weans her foal she does so gradually – not abruptly – and there is one other vital difference; in the wild, the foal has a substitute for her in the form of his peers or even his pair-bond. The simultaneous loss of both mother and equine peers verges on social deprivation akin to that which Harlow's monkeys suffered, and is a serious welfare issue which goes largely ignored by horse owners.

Such practices have lifelong consequences for horses in that they grow up more fearful and timid than their peers in the wild, not least because the separation occurs at a sensitive time in their behavioural development.

CHAPTER NINE

PLAYTIME!

After reading this chapter, you should be able to answer questions on the following:

- The importance of stretching in the new-born foal
- The functions of play in young horses
- Patterns of equine play
- The function of object play
- What factors influence when horses choose to play
- When to start training the young foal
- Using play as a training technique with the older horse

Research published a few years ago suggested that children who play often are more likely to grow up intelligent than those who play less. The study showed that certain vital areas in the brain involved in learning were increased in size when these children played often, and the result was that they became 'cleverer'.

Before I consider this point with respect to horses, ie whether playful horses are more intelligent and therefore, more trainable, I want to focus on the development of play in the young foal. From its birth to a playful six-month-old, the foal undergoes a journey from being entirely dependent on his mother, to an individual that is fully integrated in a herd. And to understand how

Most foals stretch up to 50 times a day.

perfectly, the sooner he can join the herd and be ready to escape from danger. So the stretching has the function of getting all parts of the foal's body working efficiently.

To show how serious a business this really is, most foals will stretch up to 50 times a day in the first few days of life. Sometimes, the stretching can be vigorous but on other occasions the stretching is relatively motionless and is performed almost casually. Stretching can occur whether the foal is standing or lying down and there are a huge variety of exercises which the foal puts himself through, very often with his eyes closed.

Again, it is most important that humans do not interfere with the foal's stretching process. Guiding a foal too early into walking around interferes with the foal's natural process of muscle development of which both sleeping and stretching are a critical part. Not only should the stretching be left uninterrupted, but scientific studies show that the foal should be allowed to perform these activities in a quiet and peaceful environment. Healthy, undisturbed foals stretch often and vigorously. With sick foals, or foals that are subjected to considerable amounts of stress (even inadvertently caused by humans), they either do not stretch sufficiently or, in certain cases, at all.

Striking the balance

The ultimate goal of the foal is to become a fully integrated member of the herd but in the first few days his entire focus and attention is on his mother. So how does he reach the point where at the time of natural weaning he is part of his own social group, and the loss of his mother's attentions do not cause him undue stress? In an experiment where baby rats were exposed to a variety of mildly unpleasant situations during the first four weeks of their lives, they grew up to be adults that learned more quickly, were less fearful and more inclined to explore strange environments than those that were left undisturbed. The answer to this strange phenomenon lies in a concept known as 'emotional toughening'.

If a baby rat grows up with his mother constantly at his side and then suddenly, one day she disappears, the stress of that rat will be much more acute than another baby rat whose mother might disappear for short periods of time and then always reappears. In other words, behavioural scientists have now recognised that

it achieves that, we have to return to the foal's first hours of development.

So many changes all need to happen in the brain and the body of the foal very quickly and in more-or-less the right sequence for the miracle to be realized. Foals have their first sleep in the first two or three hours of life and behavioural scientists now know that this sleep is a precursor to the first stretching behaviours that should occur within four hours. Some scientists suggest that the appearance of stretching is of utmost importance because it suggests that the foal is approaching the final level of physical competence and wellbeing. In other words, a foal that does not stretch at all has not completed the sequence of early behaviours so critical to future health, and this should give cause for grave concern.

Of course it makes sense that after many months in the womb, the muscles and tendons of the foal will be stiff, but the foal stretches for a more serious reason. The quicker he can get all limbs and other parts of his body functioning

a type of 'emotional toughening' needs to take place for an animal to grow up psychologically well-adjusted and secure. In this case, a rat has to learn that sometimes in life he will lose the animal he is most attached to, but that she always returns. That she always returns helps the young animal to feel secure.

In the same way, in nature the foal's social transition takes place gradually. As a result of these slow changes, the foal experiences emotional toughening, as well as improved physical development and co-ordination as he interacts more with other youngsters. As early as the first week of life, the foal starts to investigate other foals in the herd (remember, in the wild foals are born at around the same time) and even at this seemingly very early age, he starts to sort out, in his mind, which of the other foals could be part of his special group.

So, in essence, the foal's behavioural development is a mixture of spending time with his mother and spending time with other foals. The balance of how this time is spent depends on the age of the foal but, as he matures, he moves to a point where the majority of his time is spent with his peers, rather than his mother. This change is closely linked with the change in

distance between mother and foal. As the foal grows up, he increases the distance between himself and his mother. Behavioural scientists have suggested that in the beginning, the foal sees his mother as a secure base from which to explore his environment, but as his attention begins to focus more on his peers, the need for the secure base provided by his mother diminishes as he finds increasing, reliable security in being with other youngsters.

During this early phase in the foal's life, a foal will form a pair-bond and the association with one particular individual, as well as with the original peer group, can endure for life if left undisturbed.

The power of play

Even if you've never been lucky enough to swim with dolphins you probably know from television that dolphins are animals that often play. But, in fact, many species of animals on the planet use play as an important part of their social repertoire and horses are no exception.

With respect to behavioural development, from the time the foal starts to interact with other foals, play becomes an important and regular activity so many behavioural scientists have been intrigued by the function and purpose of play. Do horses play just because they enjoy it? By observing how horses play, which horses they play with and when they play, scientists have been able to build up a picture of the likely functions of play. We also rely to a large extent on studies of play behaviour in other young animals as sometimes these can give us insights into why horses play. For instance, it was found that hungry kittens played with each other more often and more boisterously than those that were well-fed. On the face of it, this seems to be a counter-productive strategy as one would expect that the kittens would choose to conserve energy, rather than spend it, when food was in short supply. But, in fact, the reverse is true because hungry kittens need to practise their hunting skills urgently if they are to survive by eating again. The theory behind feline play, therefore, is that play has a very important function of allowing young animals to practise survival skills which, in the case of kittens, is hunting behaviour. Horses, too, practise survival skills by playing in mock fights with each other, or running games designed to test escape skills in the face of danger.

We now know that horse play is not an aimless activity and, in fact, a number of patterns in play have been observed. These patterns are innate – in other words, the foal does not need to learn the patterns, he is born knowing them – but of course, how skilled he becomes at them is a direct result of practice, and so young horses play often.

FOAL PLAY PATTERNS
Chase and charge
One horse will signal his desire of wanting to play by setting off on his own in a canter across the field. Another horse will join in by chasing the first one, and often this causes the whole group to set off together. Chase and charge games tend to be characterized by running in a specific direction.

Nip and shove
This is play that takes place between two individuals and is a form of play-fighting. Nip and shove games help young male horses practise their skills which will be important when they are older stallions challenging or protecting the right to reproduce with the mares.

Play-mounting
Young colts start by mounting their mothers but soon change to mounting other youngsters. Interestingly, stallions are surprisingly tolerant of this type of play and it is only the completely under-socialised, maladjusted domestic stallion that might be guilty of stamping on youngsters and killing them.

Object play
This is where a horse plays alone with an object such as a branch or a stone. Some behavioural scientists have suggested that too much object play in a horse is a sign that the horse lacks equine company, and certainly many of us could probably think of examples of stabled horses

Chase and charge!

Nip and shove!

that spend hours every day playing with the bolt on their stable doors. Such suggestions have not yet been scientifically proven, but owners would probably do well to at least review their horse's regime in terms of social contact.

In the wild, object play fulfills one very important function in that horses learn that unusual but unthreatening objects do not need to be feared and can even be played with. So, whilst suspicion of novel objects is a good strategy in the young horse, as he matures, he learns that there are many things in the environment that are not dangerous, and he does some of this learning through play. Without this ability to learn that some things are dangerous and some are not, the horse would grow up fearful of everything and would eventually collapse, exhausted.

As well as helping the foal to practise survival skills, what other functions does play have in the horse?

■ In the young horse, play improves blood supply around the body and is thus a crucial part of a young horse reaching peak physical performance.

■ Play helps herd cohesion and strengthens bonds between individuals.
■ Play also helps horses learn to interact appropriately with each other. Without play, social manners may never fully develop.

The research which suggests that children who play often are clever and do better at school is relevant to horses because it is likely that a playful horse will also grow up better equipped to deal with other horses and his environment than one denied access to play.

What influences when to play and for how long?

There are a number of things that affect how often horses play and the most important of these is age and gender. Quite simply, younger horses play much more than adult horses do and colts play more than fillies. In studies of the difference between lengths of playtime in New Forest ponies, colts played almost twice as much as fillies did, and ethologists have suggested that the main reason for this is because colts will grow up into adults that will want to challenge a stallion for the right to reproduce with the mares. So the skills of the colts have to be better than those of the fillies and so more practice is necessary.

Weather conditions are also all-important. Young horses do not play unless the conditions are perfect. What is perfect from the horse's point of view, is when the weather conditions allow the horse to feel safe. Frightened horses do not play. If a horse were to indulge in boisterous play whilst the wind was howling around him, he would be even less likely to hear an approaching predator. Add this to the fact that his attention has been diverted away from thinking about danger and onto his playmate, and it starts to become obvious that the right conditions are essential for play to occur.

The younger they start, the easier it is for foals, like humans, to learn.

Although you now know from the previous chapter of the potential dangers of 'foal imprinting' or invasive handling in the few hours surrounding the foals' birth, outside of the critical first few days it is entirely acceptable to introduce some basic handling of the foal. Many scientific studies of different animals show that animals do indeed learn best when they are young, and turning away a youngster for three years and then suddenly starting his training does not make biological sense and may cause the horse to become anxious and fearful.

Using play in training

If you own a dog then you probably just automatically start playing and clowning around with him several times a day. But most of us have no idea where to start when it comes to playing with horses; perhaps some of us have not even dreamt it was possible to do so. But potentially, horses have the edge over dogs in that they are born with innate play patterns which I described above – ready-made games, in other words, just ripe for the taking.

Perhaps the reason horse play as a training technique has been so little understood until now is because dog and cat play primarily revolves around the development of hunting skills – skills that are more recognisable to us. The kitten that looks so cute as it pounces and bats a ball of string around is really just fine-tuning its hunting skills. And the dog that runs after a ball and retrieves it for you is also just honing his predatory chase-and-kill behaviours.

Training benefits

By introducing one or more of the equine play patterns into training sessions, our time with our horses becomes both more fulfilling and mutually rewarding. And when we encounter problems in training our horse, we can intersperse training with play, thus opening up the horse's mind more quickly to new ideas.

Remember the research revealed that children who played most were the most likely to achieve top marks at school. So one of the most important things to remember if you have a problem with your horse is to lighten up! As soon as it is practical and safe to do so, start incorporating play into the training. Not only will your horse be more clever, your problem is likely to be solved far sooner, also.

A quick fix?

Your horse nips you constantly whilst you try to groom. Perhaps your horse is just trying to play with you. Direct his behaviour onto something more appropriate – here at the Natural Animal Centre, we encourage horse Jessica to play with the objects in her toy box whilst she is being groomed (see Chapter One for more on horse toy boxes).

CHAPTER TEN

FAMILY MATTERS

After reading this chapter, you should be able to answer questions on the following:

■ Why studying zebra behaviour can be helpful in analysing horse behaviour
■ Why stallions, not mares, self-mutilate
■ The role of the stallion as protector
■ The role of the stallion as play-mate
■ The sexual behaviours of the stallion
■ Why only one stallion actually mates
■ Welfare concerns with respect to the domestic 'teaser' stallion

One of the things that you really notice when you are in the African savannah amongst herds of zebra, is what fantastically good parents zebras are to their young. Even if you are not specifically looking for this kind of behaviour you cannot help noticing it because the zebras are so attentive, so watchful, so reactive and playful with their foals.

Zebras (and in particular the Plains – or Burchell's – Zebra) are closely related to the domestic horse and one of the reasons Ross and I take three or four trips a year to study them is because we can learn so much about the behaviour of the domestic horse by comparing them to zebras.

In our view, the zebra represents one of the last, truly wild groups of equids that can be studied just as they really are and have been in history. Even the so-called wild mustangs of North America are, in actual fact, feral horses and nowadays, they are increasingly interfered with and managed by humans.

Burchell's Zebra, truly wild!

Are horses good parents?

The question of whether domestic horses make good parents (or not) is not something that comes up very often, I find. We are more used to hearing people talk about which genes (or 'lines') the stallion is imparting to the foal, and many brood mares are relegated to being little more than a living receptacle for carrying the unborn foal for several months. In my experience, the role of the stallion as parent is hardly considered at all, whilst the role of the mare as parent is generally restricted to the biological function of nursing within the shortest possible time before the foal is weaned.

Yet, is this a complete picture? The enormous number of studies performed by behavioural scientists on horses in the wild, as well as our findings of the behaviour of parent zebras, suggests that we are, perhaps, ignoring one of the most fundamental truths when it comes to the way we breed and rear our horses.

Work done over 60 years ago by human psychologists showed that children who lost their parents and were raised in institutions were, on average, disadvantaged with respect to physical, mental and emotional development. That these findings are true of horses also is undeniable – without parents, horses too grow up similarly adversely affected. So isn't it about time that horse owners caught up with human psychologists and started realising that the eight-year-old gelding they were about to buy did not just arrive from outer space as a ready-made adult, but that he is a product of both his parents' genes and the time they both invested in him? It remains uncommon for mares and stallions to be allowed to live together in a permanent herd so that courtship behaviours can be acted out and, even more importantly, so that parenting duties can be shared. Yet, when we have observed zebra parents it is clear that a system of division of duties prevails.

It is important, therefore, for us horse owners to understand that to deny horses the opportunity to act as parents not only deprives them of one of their most important, natural drivers in life, but is also a welfare issue for the young foal who relies on one or both parents at different stages in his behavioural development.

Self-mutilation

One of the most disturbing behavioural cases I have ever been involved in concerned a stallion that was self-mutilating to such an extent that he had chewed a large hole, the size of a man's fist, on either side of his flanks. The incidence of self-mutilation in stallions is considerably higher than that in mares; in fact, it is rare to hear of a mare that is behaving so compulsively and harmfully towards herself.

Most behavioural scientists agree that it is being stabled that causes self-mutilation in stallions – it is a reflection of his failure to cope with his environment. But thousands of mares are housed in similar conditions yet they do not resort to self-mutilation, so there must be something else happening which prevents the stallion adapting to his circumstances less well overall.

There are two main reasons that are typically given for the stallion's behaviour:

- A stallion kept for the purposes of copulation only, and is never given the opportunity to interact with his young, becomes chronically stressed to the point of exhibiting self-harm.
- A stallion that is not given the opportunity to remain with both mares and other stallions is denied, arguably, the ability to act out his most significant of social needs – being part of a group.

Wild fathers

So what sort of life does the father stallion lead in the wild? Are stallions really the rampaging, sex-crazed animals they are so famous for? On the contrary, research shows that sex is only a part of the question. It is true that alpha stallions will mate with all the mares in the herd, giving no other males a look-in, but there is another aspect to stallion reproductive behaviour which is seldom discussed. Even after mating has occurred, the stallion and mare will closely associate together for days. Stallions have been seen to maintain close body contact with the mare as he grazes alongside her, and will also show 'chinning' behaviour by resting his chin on her rump for long periods.

The idea that a stallion would mate and then more-or-less disappear out of the mare's life until she was next in season is false, and ethologists have suggested that the main purpose of stallion and mare continuing to consort closely together after mating is to allow a new form of bonding to occur – the kind that would best prepare them for the joint parenting

After mating, the stallion and mare will closely associate together for days.

duties that are to follow.

So stallions at stud that are brought in merely to provide sperm and are then given no further access to the mare, are being denied the first important part of acting out behaviours that relate to becoming a father.

The stallion as protector

Many mares leave the herd to give birth and it is at this time that the stallion's role becomes critical. Whilst the mare is vulnerable – in labour or giving birth – the stallion begins the role which is to become a key one for him over the next few months, that of protector. The stallion ensures that the new mother is neither disturbed by other horses in the herd, nor attacked by predators. Indeed, stallions have been known to actually attack animals, such as lions, at this time, an indication of how strong their parental drive as protector is.

Once the foal is born and joins the herd with its mother, then its protection is shared by the herd as a whole:

■ The mare offers the first bastion of protection by virtue of always being in close proximity to the foal.

■ The alpha stallion offers protection, not only by keeping close to the foal, but also by being on red-alert for predators almost all the time. In this way, the stallion allows the mare to be off-duty for some of the time, a circumstance that is usually denied brood mares in a domestic setting.

■ The bachelor stallions on the periphery of the nursery herd form a cordon of protection around all the mares and foals.

When the herd is attacked by predators, foals are herded into the middle of the group away from danger on the sidelines, and the whole herd gallops away from the predators at the speed of the slowest foal. As a result, many stallions end up giving their lives for protection of foals that they did not even sire – the ultimate sacrifice as they could, in theory, easily gallop away from danger at top speed.

This fundamental drive to protect the herd is what causes so much unhappiness for the solitary, stabled stallion – stallions are biologically programmed to perform these behaviours and it is for this reason that behaviourists believe it is so limiting to see the stallion's role as provider of sperm only.

Batchelor stallions invest considerable time in playing with young foals.

Child's play

Our research on zebras has repeatedly shown that the relationship of the stallion with his offspring also extends to include play. Other behavioural research performed on wild horses has shown that stallions will invest time in playing with their own progeny in preference to others. Play is an important part of learning and exploration in the young foal and it makes sense, from an evolutionary perspective, that the foal learns to play with its father.

Interestingly, the bachelor stallions also invest considerable time in playing with all the young foals. In fact, when we observe zebra bachelor herds, we often get side-tracked by what is happening; it seems like all the real action is happening there as they encourage youngsters – particularly other young colts – to interact and play with them.

Owners of young stallions often report that it is the play behaviour of these horses that motivates them to keep them entire – after all, this is arguably the best side of the stallion as far as humans are concerned.

Three steps to fatherhood

There are three main behaviours in the alpha stallion's sexual behavioural repertoire:

Challenging or not . .

Contests between stallions are performed to ascertain which horse has the highest sexual status within the overall hierarchy of the herd – and the ultimate opportunity to mate with the mares. The challenges are always performed on a one-to-one basis and bachelor stallions, perceiving they have little chance of toppling a reigning alpha stallion, will not even attempt to compete. The risk of injury in such a one-sided contest (which may be followed by death from a predator) is simply too high. Thus, the decisions made by the majority of the stallions not to challenge is an important part of sexual behaviour in horses and a crucial element in maintaining bonds and co-operative behaviour within the herd.

However, if a stallion believes the risk of possible injury is outweighed by the likely outcome of winning alpha status, then he will challenge the existing alpha stallion. Interestingly, the secretion of the hormone testosterone in bachelor stallions is said to be linked not just to preparation for mating with the mares, but also to the stallion's determination to win a particular contest.

Under most domestic conditions, these normal and natural contesting behaviours are completely denied in bachelor stallions.

Sign-posting or marking

Most horse owners know that stallions claim their home ranges by urinating and defecating in preferred, selected areas. This behaviour is known as sign-posting but does, in fact, have the double purpose of both staking out territory, and encouraging mare sexual behaviour through the depositing of pheromones (chemicals) found in the stallion's urine and droppings.

Mating

One of the oddest behaviours of all hoofed animals – except the pig – is the olfactory reflex called *flehmen*. In this behaviour, the stallion fully extends his neck, closes his nostrils and raises his upper lip whilst taking in shallow breaths. For many years, behavioural scientists have known that *flehmen* is a response to mare urine and that it functions as a form of odour testing. More recent research, however, shows that other senses beyond that of smell may also be involved as *flehmen* also occurs in the stallion in response to sounds made by the mare, such as low-pitched knickering or touch behaviours between the two, such as nudging.

Welfare concerns about a stallion that is kept continuously in a stable at stud and is brought out only when he is used as a 'teaser'.

This is the reverse situation of the above. Here we have a stallion that is (artificially) denied the opportunity to mate but is not given the biological possibility of suppressing his libido by being allowed to live in a large group of other male horses. In the wild, he would be given the opportunity to choose whether to compete with the alpha stallion – or not.

The cost on both the body of the 'teaser' and on his emotional state (of continually producing hormones for a purpose that is repeatedly frustrated) can be very high indeed and, from a purely behavioural perspective, many of these stallions become increasingly aggressive and difficult to handle. The important thing for us to realize is that this is a purely man-made behaviour – nature has not designed the bachelor stallion to behave in this way.

A horse exhibiting the olfactory reflex known as the flehmen.

Close groupings of males in bachelor herds are an indication of successful adaption in the horse.

FURTHER THOUGHTS ON STALLION BEHAVIOUR

If only one alpha stallion mates with all the mares in the herd, are all the other stallions aggressive, frustrated and sex starved, showing all those behaviour problems for which the domestic stallion has become so notorious? Libido is the term given by behavioural scientists to displays of sexual behaviour. So whilst we have been fed images of high libido stallions, the reality is that by far the majority of male horses, zebras and many other hooved animals are characterised by long periods of complete absence of libido – in other words, complete loss of sex drive.

Because of the way the equine social structure works – one alpha stallion only serves all the mares – the grouping together of the so-called 'bachelor' stallions on the periphery of the main nursery herd functions as a biological means of suppressing libido in individual males. Clearly, this makes sense when you think about it. If you were not likely to get a chance to mate with a mare for many years, then it would be a waste of time and energy (ie biologically maladaptive) to keep producing hormones that prepared you for mating. In this sense, we know that close groupings of males in bachelor herds are actually an indication of successful adaption in the horse.

CHAPTER ELEVEN

MUM'S THE WORD

After reading this chapter, you should be able to answer questions on the following:

- That animals learn before they are even born
- Why pregnant mares should be kept free from stress
- Why the Positive Horse Magic clicker training system is helpful to pregnant mares
- The four key aspects of Attachment Theory in understanding mare-foal bonding

In the last chapter, I wrote that the role of the stallion as parent involves more than simply imparting his genes to his offspring. In the wild, stallions also play a pivotal, crucial role in protection of the foals. What factors cause one stallion to rise to alpha status above another has as much to do with his ability to protect both mares and foals at times when they are most vulnerable to predation, as it has to do with 'good' genes. After all, no mare would agree to reproduce with a stallion that does not offer a superior protection service. It would not make sense for her to waste nearly a year of her life in pregnancy, only to lose her foal quickly because the father did not help her when her foal was at its weakest.

On the other hand, of course, we are all much more familiar with the role of the mare as mother. Clearly, as the one carrying the unborn baby foal there is no question that she is going beyond the role of just imparting her genes. The fact that horses are a species that relies on the maternal bond for healthy behavioural development in the foal means that input – or nurture – from the mare is both obvious and essential.

Pre-birth learning

Studies performed on other animals like rats and dogs have shown that learning in the new-born animal does not start at the time of birth but, in fact, begins while the baby is developing in the mother's uterus. In the Fifties, pregnant mother rats were subjected to a number of stressful events and their unborn babies grew up to be more emotional and more reactive to stress after they were born.

For instance, if their mother jumped at a loud noise whilst she was pregnant then later on, the new-born baby rats were proven to became emotionally stressed too when they heard the same, loud noise.

How was this happening? Well, before birth,

Relaxed dams make for relaxed foals.

the baby rats had leaned to recognise the stress hormones secreted in the mother's body when she reacted to something fearful, which means that learning was actually taking place between mother and unborn babies through the placenta.

Interestingly, the reverse of this experiment was tested on human mothers in the 1980's – pregnant mothers were played calming, melodious music at the same time every day and the babies were proven to be able to transfer the positive learning they had undergone before they were born, to life after birth. Whenever they cried, the same music was played to them with a corresponding, calming effect.

Although similar studies have not yet been performed on unborn foals, we can safely assume that trans-placental learning takes place between mare and unborn foal, as well. This is because the parts of the brain and other glands in the body that are responsible for stimulating (or suppressing) fear, aggression and stress are pretty much the same in all animals, regardless of whether they are a rat or a horse.

If foals are learning from their mothers before they are even born, does this mean extra responsibilities for the owner of a pregnant mare?

Yes! It is important to realise that the minds of foals are not the blank sheet of paper that so many people imagine them to be. Other experiments on pregnant rats and their new-born babies showed that baby rats showed the same preferences and aversions for certain foods that their mothers had showed during pregnancy, so the question of learning between mother and unborn baby is really undoubted.

In later studies performed on dogs, scientists proved that puppies that were born to stressed mothers came into the world with a high level of stress already – even though they had only just been born! This is an important study for horse owners; clearly, we can help the situation by making sure the pregnant mare undergoes as little stress as possible during pregnancy. Similarly, choosing NOT to breed from an over-reactive, easily stressed mare can be a good decision for any prospective offspring. This is because, outside of any genetic input, an overly nervous mare is actually teaching her unborn foal to be stressed and anxious too.

One of the easiest ways to relieve stress in the pregnant mare is to turn her out in company for as much as possible. Remember, in the wild the mare has the support of other mares around her, as well as the protection of the stallions. A pregnant mare stabled alone for long hours is not only physically restricted – which causes stress in itself – but is also suffering from social isolation at a time when, arguably, she most needs the companionship of other horses.

Turning out pregnant mares with the stallions which have sired their offspring makes the most perfect sense of all – such management arrangements not only fulfil a parental need in the stallion, but the stallion's presence can enhance emotional well-being in the mare, and the knock-on effect is a calmer, more psychologically well-adjusted new-born foal.

If socialising with the stallion is not an option for some reason, then make sure that the pregnant mare is turned out with other companions. In the wild, pregnant mares prepare for the birth of their foals by forming nursery groups, so turnout with other pregnant mares is helpful. Even geldings can play a role as surrogate mothers because, in the wild, bachelors would offer peripheral companionship and support to the expectant mares.

If you handled or trained a pregnant mare using clicker training (which we use in our Positive Horse Magic training) would you be helping the development of calm emotions in her unborn foal?

Studies on both rats and dogs showed that unborn babies learned to react in the same way their mothers did to various stimuli in the environment, regardless of whether the stimulus caused a positive or negative experience. It goes without saying, therefore, that if a pregnant mare experienced stressful handling or training whilst she was pregnant, then the likelihood of her foal being born more emotional and over-reactive than usual is very high indeed.

Because clicker training is a pleasant experience for the mare – she earns a reward for performing the desired behaviour through the use of positive reinforcement – she will transfer the positive experience to her unborn foal, and the foal is likely to be born calmer and less emotionally reactive to handling by humans when the appropriate time for introduction to humans comes.

Through early bonding a foal learns to recognise his mother.

Early bonding between mare and foal

You will remember from Chapter Eight that, strictly speaking, imprinting or bonding between mother and baby occurs mainly in birds. But the term is now generally accepted as being a phenomenon that describes early bonding in other species of animals also, particularly where the risk of a baby bonding to the wrong animal is possible. So mares minimise this risk first of all by separating from the herd at the time of birth (young mares do not necessarily do this, however), so that the new-born foal should, literally, only have eyes (and of course, ears and a nose) for them.

The function of imprinting has been well-studied and it is important to remember two things: imprinting leads to suckling but also many would say, more importantly, imprinting is about protection. Through this early and relatively rapid bonding, a foal learns to recognise his mother who will protect him and the mare, of course, bonds to her foal so that she does not invest time and energy protecting someone else's foal. That the imprinting process between mother and foal should not be interfered with (medical considerations aside) should be fairly obvious to us all. It is important that we remember that in the wild the mare and foal would not be disturbed during this crucial time, and mares have been observed chasing off curious herd members who come too close.

Bonding to the mare over the first few hours allows the foal to learn that it is a horse – because its mother is a horse. This is why there is so much concern from behavioural scientists that the newly-born foal is sometimes coerced by trainers into the most unnatural of behaviours – out of time and sequence in terms of normal behavioural development – such as being asked to trot, jump over logs, accept grooming brushes, clippers and so on.

Child psychology

In the middle of the last century, a human psychologist called John Bowlby began studying the role of bonding between babies and their mothers from a scientific perspective, and although he worked only in the human field, his work is of utmost importance to us when we try to understand the significance of parents in the young foal's life. Bowlby's research happened at a time when only purely speculative psycho-babble reigned. Because Freudian theories such as the Oedipus complex tended to be taken as undisputed starting points for understanding mother-child bonding, Bowlby's decision to look to science for the answers was practically unique at the time. But through his own discoveries, and by drawing on ethological work being performed at the same time (by Konrad Lorenz and others), he was able to come up with a number of key ideas associated with the process of bonding – or what he called, attachment – and these ideas give us much insight into how young foals should develop with the support of their mothers as well.

Key aspects of mother/baby bonding
1. Protection

The first critical point, and arguably the most important, was that the primary reason for attachment between mother and foal is to do with protection. This is, if you like, the function of attachment. If a foal did not become attached to his mother, then he would not know who to be close to when danger threatened. The mare, on the other hand, needed to become attached to her foal because she needed to learn who to protect. Clearly she neither wants to waste time, nor risk her life, for the wrong baby.

This idea of protection as a biological function of attachment was a little surprising to many people at first – it had always been thought that suckling was the first sign of attachment. But if we study the development of the foal, then we see too that suckling is fairly low down the timetable of behavioural events in the set sequence of development seen in Chapter Eight.

People who have seen foals just after they are born agree that the mare seems unhurried to encourage her foal to suckle – she spends that first hour sniffing, nickering and licking the foal herself (so that she can learn to attach to him), and the foal sniffs her and listens to her and, in so doing, learns to attach to her as well. It is often up to an hour after birth before the first suckling takes place – by which time attachment has already occurred.

This is an important concept for over-anxious, albeit extremely well-intentioned people, who try to encourage the foal to its feet (out of behavioural sequence) and make it suckle too early. Too much intervention here can even cause the opposite effect and the foal may become reluctant to suckle – this makes sense

His dam is a secure base from which the new-born foal can explore the world.

when you understand that the attachment process has been broken.

2. Proximity

Bowlby recognised that for attachment to occur there had to be proximity between mare and foal and so he said that attachment was a spatial theory, too. The space between mare and foal remains very small in the early days and weeks after the foal is born. One of the ways that this spatial theory is tested is, of course, to observe what happens when a mother animal is separated from her baby – there is always considerable distress on both sides. The level of stress shown is an indication to us of how important proximity to the mother is to the baby animal.

Observations of wild horses have shown that being close to the mare is a behaviour that young foals show for up to two years or more of age. This means that taking foals away from their mothers – often at around six months of age – causes a massive breakdown in the attachment process and, of course, places the foal at huge risk of growing up psychologically maladjusted.

3. Separation

In later studies not performed by Bowlby himself, other psychologists proved that the role of the mother during the development of attachment also includes the idea that she is a secure base from which to explore the world. How human toddlers coped when their mothers left them for a very short period of time, and how they reacted to her at the time of reunion, gives us some very important clues about how attachment works for the mare and foal, too. In the human studies, mothers and toddlers played together in a room and then the mother was asked to leave the toddler alone for a couple of minutes. Some toddlers continued to play quietly with their toys but others seemed unable to continue and cried a lot. On the return of the mothers, some babies greeted their mothers lovingly and resumed playing (this group became known as the secure-attached group, implying that they could cope in a well-adjusted way with brief separations from their mother). But many of the toddlers shunned their mothers when they returned or showed a mix of both shunning and greeting. Psychologists were able to conclude that they toddlers were insecure in their attachments.

These studies show that the secure babies apparently all believed that their mother would come back, and this was reflected in their behaviour of continuing to play. But the insecure babies did not know what would happen when their mothers left them, and so their behaviours became more disorganised and distressed.

This research is of great significance to us as horse owners. If foals are separated from their mothers too early, they grow up insecure and, just like their human counterparts, we see suppression of normal play and exploratory behaviours. Unfortunately, the more the latter are suppressed, the less opportunity the foal has for normal development, with long-term adverse consequences.

For some foals however, separation from their mothers only happens once – traumatically and forever. This abrupt severing of attachment because of artificial weaning practices and misplaced human belief goes far beyond what the human studies showed. As horse owners, we should be aware that this common approach to separation of mare and foal can create permanent psychological damage because it is so traumatic and goes beyond anything nature ever intended.

4. History

The last theory to discuss in the development of attachment is the notion that current bonding between mother and baby is affected by the mother's own attachment history. This means that if the mare did not bond properly to her own mother, then she would have grown up insecure herself. As a result, her insecurities from her personal attachment history are reflected in her ability to attach to her own foal who, in turn, is likely to grow up insecure as well.

Tales of aggression or even rejection of their foals by mares are, unfortunately, all too common and, health considerations aside, we would do well to look at the attachment history of such a mare before breeding from her again.

By ignoring this important truth, we risk producing generation after generation of nervous, insecure young horses which, without help, remain in this state for all of their lives. And that situation is, without question, a welfare problem which is, sadly, often ignored.

CHAPTER TWELVE

LEARNING TO BE BRAVE

After reading this chapter, you should be able to answer questions on the following:

- The sensitive phase of early learning
- Why under-socialised and poorly habituated horses suffer from poor welfare
- When the sensitive phase is likely to occur in young horses
- The correct definitions of fear, phobia, anxiety and displacement
- The meaning of flooding
- Why the use of flooding as a training technique causes welfare problems for the horse

Dog owners show the way

For more than a decade, it has been common practice for owners of young puppies to take their animals to 'socialisation' classes or 'puppy parties'. (Socialisation is the phrase used to describe the process whereby, amongst other things, an animal learns appropriate social behaviour.) So a puppy will go to a socialisation class to have the opportunity to learn how to interact with other dogs and to get used to being approached by different kinds of people. Interestingly, we know it is possible for a number of animals, including dogs, cats and horses, to undergo a process of socialisation with their own species at the same time as they are being socialised to humans.

Canine behavioural scientists know there is a sensitive phase in the development of the puppy

Ground-breaking research in the 1960's showed scientists how dogs learn about the world around them. It also showed scientists when canine brains are best equipped to carry out that learning process. Even at that stage, there was a recognition that animals seemed to go through phases of behavioural and learning development and scientists wanted to know whether it mattered when an animal first learnt about something. From here, it was a short step to work out whether they could teach an old dog new tricks!

By performing a number of experiments on a variety of breeds, they proved the old adage that what an animal learns first, it learns best. For instance, puppies that were reared in social isolation developed into adult dogs which were fearful and withdrawn in the company of other dogs. On the other hand, kittens that were raised in an enriched, stimulating environment were better at solving puzzles. Both species were easier to train when appropriately socialised with other animals of their own species, as well as with human beings.

For dogs to live successfully with humans they need to socialise both with their own kind, and with humans.

Horses benefit from socialising with humans, too!

when it is most open to learning (approximately six to 12 weeks of age). These owners gently and gradually expose their puppies during this time to the things in life they want them to cope with as adults. As a result, their puppies have the best chance of growing up to be psychologically well adjusted. So, for example, if you wanted your adult dog to go to a busy market with you every weekend, then you would expose the puppy to short, frequent visits to the market, allowing it to meet as many different people as possible, and gradually get it used to the novel situation.

Both socialisation and habituation (getting used to potentially threatening things) is thus essential for a puppy to grow up into a psychologically well-adjusted adult dog. Without it, the puppy develops into a distrusting animal that is difficult to train and shows inappropriate behaviour towards other dogs and people.

Yet even though socialisation is now a widely accepted practice amongst dog owners, this is a concept that is seldom discussed when it comes to horses. Vets actively encourage puppy owners to attend puppy parties at their surgeries, yet it is practically unheard of for

clients to be advised of the benefits of socialisation for the horse. If anything, some people actively separate horses from people (turn them away) during those early years, with the result that many horses receive only minimal contact with humans.

Social skills

Given that for thousands of years man and horse have shared an uneasy relationship, it would seem that we horse owners should be working even harder than puppy owners to socialise our horses to humans! Without adequate socialisation, the horse quickly learns to view man as a potential, persistent threat.

Add to this all the thousands of other things in the environment that the horse finds threatening – from hoses to pigs to traffic – and it is little wonder that so many of us end up feeling frustrated with our spooky horses! Because we know that puppies that are well-socialised are easier to train, it seems grossly remiss that socialisation of the horse is not standard practice, particularly when so many riders acquire horses because of their very desire to train them.

Ignoring the socialisation of the horse means his welfare is impaired. An under-socialised, poorly habituated horse can never relax, his life is full of threatening things to which he never becomes accustomed, and he becomes subject to chronic stress. On a seemingly never-ending treadmill, he finds it increasingly harder to learn and his day-to-day behaviour becomes more and more random and disorganised. Ultimately, his health is compromised as he becomes more susceptible to infection and other immune-mediated problems such as allergies, respiratory disorders, skin sensitivities and so on. Vets have even reported that under-socialised dogs take longer to recover from operations or illness and whilst this has not yet been tested in horses, it seems reasonable to assume that as horses have similar physiological responses to stress as dogs, then they would also suffer from slow recovery rates.

The best time to learn

The exact socialisation period of the horse, when it is most sensitive to learning appropriate social behaviour, has not been worked out scientifically, but we can try to make deductions by looking at other animals. In cats and dogs, the sensitive phase happens:

- before these animals are sexually mature and
- before they are most likely as youngsters to react fearfully to new things (in dogs, this time is roughly recognised as being after 12 weeks of age).

So one could suggest with some confidence that the sensitive socialisation period of the horse would occur sometime during the first year (before it became sexually mature). Ethologists have also suggested that before the age of six months the young horse is curious and relatively fearless about new things it encounters in the environment. After this, novel experiences are viewed with suspicion, even fear.

So our current behavioural knowledge of horses suggests that horses need to be socialised to people and other horses before they are six months of age! At the same time, we know that this is also the period when they learn most about the environment around them so we should also be introducing and habituating them to all the things we want them to cope with in adult life (like going into a trailer, or being examined by a vet).

Before six months of age, young horses are curious and relatively fearless – exploring their surroundings with curiousity.

Far from ideal

How far does common practice seem to be from the scientific facts for healthy equine development? Leading the average young horse down the road when he is two or three years old in an effort to get him to get him used to traffic is often the only overt attempt at 'socialising' him – and of course, such practice is way too late in terms of the sensitive phase. That is not to say that the adult horse is unable to learn about things after the sensitive socialisation age, but just that this is the time when he is most receptive to learning about new things. Simply put, this is the easiest time for him to take in new information. Think about children who are easily able to learn a second or third language when they are very young, and compare that to how many classes the average adult has to take to achieve only a faltering acquisition of a foreign tongue.

Insufficient socialisation of the horse not only leads to long-term psychological maladjustment, but sometimes to the most drastic of actions being taken by owners whose horse's behaviour develops into the unacceptable in adult life. Socialising your horse adequately, even if he is already in adulthood, could literally be a life-saving practice. Also, being aware of things that you and I take for granted but that are threatening to horses is the first step in trying to build a habituation programme for your horse that will help him develop into a happy and confident animal.

Fear – the facts

The most common result of lack of adequate socialisation is a fearful adult horse, so it is important that we truly understand the meaning of the word fear. Riders tend to loosely and indiscriminately use certain phrases such as, "my horse is phobic about cows," or "anxious of going out with other horses," without true understanding of the terms. But, in fact, much research into human fears has enabled behavioural scientists to prepare a fairly precise categorisation of the different types of nervousness in the horse as follows:

1. Fear – a feeling of apprehension associated with the presence or proximity of an object, an individual or social situation. Common examples for horses are fear of:
■ Animals such as dogs and sheep.

Your horse may be fearful of a trailer or horsebox.

■ The bit (or other parts of tack, like the girth).
■ The lorry or trailer.
■ The vet or the dentist.
■ Even other horses.

2. Phobia – a profound and quickly developed fear reaction that does not cease with gradual exposure to the object (as ordinary fears do) over time. Common examples for horses are, phobia of:
■ Fireworks.
■ Pigs.
■ Trailers.

3. Anxiety – the apprehensive anticipation of future danger or misfortune accompanied by tension, activity and vigilance. There are many different kinds of anxiety including:
■ Separation anxiety – the behaviours the horse displays when his pair-bond is about to be removed.
■ Displacements – the behaviours the horse displays when it is about to be loaded into the trailer, for example, pawing the ground or head tossing. Sometimes, displacements can be associated with confusion and nervousness simply because the horse does not understand what it is being asked to learn.

Clearly, understanding that the horse which runs to the gate when its friend is taken away is suffering from separation anxiety, and not just trying to be naughty or get its own way, will have an impact on what action you decide to take to deal with the situation. Similarly, rough, forceful

Horses may be subjected to separation anxiety when their pair-bond is taken from the field.

Flooding fears

Unfortunately, where the emphasis in puppy socialisation has been on gradual exposure of the animal to something new, such practices are rare when it comes to training horses. Horse training usually forces the (typically) under-socialised, poorly-habituated horse to confront his fears, sometimes using a technique known as flooding. Flooding is where a horse (or any animal or human, for that matter) is forced to remain in the proximity of something it fears AND is given no opportunity for escape. Psychologists have shown that pronounced, prolonged presentation of the frightening thing, with no opportunity to alleviate the fear (ie move away), can cause profound psychological damage to the horse with a long-lasting phobic response. To give an example, the suggestion of putting a horse that is fearful of pigs into a stable with a pig and leaving them overnight "to get on with it," is not only scientifically flawed but potentially dangerous to the horse (not to mention the welfare of the poor pig!).

handling of the horse at the time of training when it meets a pig out on a hack could not only result in the creation of fear of pigs, but even phobic behaviour that is much harder to unravel.

Experiments performed on people who were flooded in the 1940's and 1950's showed that flooding had a dubious success record and when it failed, which it usually did, psychological damage was severe and long-lasting.

A phobia of pigs can be overcome!

How not to train horses!

Flooding of horses is, unfortunately, common. Stories abound of routine flooding of the horse to force it on to a trailer, or flooding it to walk past a parked tractor. I have personally witnessed some of the so-called top horsemen in the world casually flood a horse for hours by kicking balls at it (to train it to accept movement of strange objects) or, alternatively, flood acceptance of being tied up by tying the horse to a post for eight to 10 hours on end.

Most puppy owners would be horrified if their dog trainer made similar suggestions at a puppy party – with good cause, because flooding of animals is both unethical, psychologically damaging and usually unsuccessful. Even if the horse has not been introduced to new things as a youngster, it is still possible throughout its adult life to continue to teach the adult horse to accept novelty – in an ethically acceptable way.

At the Natural Animal Centre, we aim to develop the understanding that so much of the horse's unwanted behaviour is a result of being motivated by fear. Unfortunately, it is still very common to hear riders talk of their horse as being 'naughty', 'stubborn', 'pig-headed' and so on, without due consideration for the horse's true behavioural motivation, and rarely with any understanding of the effects of lack of socialisation and habituation in the adult horse.

It is possible to teach horses to accept novelty in an ethically acceptable way.

PART THREE

CHAPTER THIRTEEN

FIELD TRAUMA

After reading this chapter, you should be able to answer questions on the following:

- How an equine behaviour consultation works
- Classical conditioning, using simple terms
- Classical conditioning, using the scientific terminology of learning theory
- The difference between a Conditioned Response and a Conditioned Emotional Response
- Why the mare in this case developed a Conditional Emotional Response to the field
- How to solve the problem

The stable: Inky's favourite place.

Angela McCrickard keeps two horses, Inky and Jerry, at her beautiful home in Sussex. A few years ago, she purchased Inky, an Arabian mare now in her 20's, as a companion for her Thoroughbred gelding Jerry, who is about 16 years old. But when Angela called me out for a behaviour consultation for Inky, she was very distressed. Inky had developed a strong dislike to being turned out in the field – she would spend almost all the time pacing up and down the fence line, she would not graze or drink in the field and, of course, she was no longer being a satisfactory

companion for Jerry. Angela was at her wits' end. All Inky seemed to want to do was live in her stable.

When she asked other people what they thought she should do, the suggestion was unanimous: leave Inky out in the field until she got over the problem (you now know from the previous chapter, that this would have been 'flooding'). But, fortunately for Inky, Angela was reluctant to go down this route as the mare was clearly unhappy in the field, even for very short periods of time. Angela asked her vet for advice and she suggested that Angela get qualified behavioural assistance. Had Angela not done so, and had she followed the advice of leaving Inky turned out permanently, the consequences for the mare could have been considerably worsened behaviour.

Ask the expert

Most dog owners are aware that if they want to improve or modify a dog's behaviour they can seek out behavioural assistance, but such approaches remain relatively rare in the horse industry. Many horse owners whose horses have problems are often caught in a situation where their vet is unable to help (most vets have not had any scientific behavioural training) and where their trainer can do little either; so it was fortuitous that the vet suggested consulting an equine behavioural scientist (*see page 98).

So what is involved in an equine behaviour consultation? In essence, it has two parts:

- An assessment of the horse.
- Some proposals for modifying the horse's behaviour.

Assessments involve asking the owner a series of questions, sometimes criss-crossing back and forth through the horse's life and daily routine, as the behavioural scientist tries to find the common thread that underlies the problem. During this part of the consultation, I always try to explore and seek out as much detail as I can to build up a behavioural profile of the horse. Only once this process is complete, would I move to the next phase and make suggestions for modifying behaviour in the horse.

Field trauma

It became clear during the consultation that Inky had suddenly become unhappy in the field. This had not always been the case and with prompting, Angela remembered one particular

> ### INKY'S CASE NOTES
> Before Angela purchased Inky, the horse had spent the majority of her life as a brood mare, having been injured when young in a race. For whatever reason (Angela did not have a complete history of Inky's life prior to purchase), Inky was not very well socialised to people and had always seemed nervous to Angela. Such nervousness seemed to pervade her life. Inky was not particularly easy to groom, was often tricky to catch and always seemed to be on edge. Her behaviour with Jerry was similar and she had not really settled down into a relaxed companionable state with him, either.
>
> Such long-term nervousness has long been recognised in humans as a root cause of chronic stress and the situation is no different with horses. In the horse, the pituitary gland (and other parts of the body that form the endocrine system) secrete hormones to help them cope with this stress and, under certain conditions, it is possible to measure how stressed a horse is by analysing these hormone levels in the bloodstream. After discussing the situation with Angela, however, I decided in Inky's case that it was not necessary to have a laboratory test to prove that Inky was stressed. Her behaviour was enough evidence that this was the case.

incident when she had gone to the field to bring the horses back to the yard and found all the electric tape down as though a horse had run through it. Inky had been highly agitated and all her subsequent behaviour was traceable back to this incident. What had prompted her to run through the electric tape, we will never know – it could have been a car backfiring as it passed her paddock, a strange dog coming into the field and chasing her – in fact, anything that would have caused her to panic and run. But before I explain why Inky had not simply got over the electric fence experience (and why flooding her by leaving her in the field would not have eased her stress), let's take a step back.

Pavlov explained

In 1928, Ivan Pavlov was studying the human digestive process – by doing experiments on dogs. Inadvertently, he made a discovery that was to forever change the way we understand how humans and animals learn. He noticed that when he went to offer food to the dogs, they started to salivate. He then pressed a buzzer prior to the food arriving and noticed that the dogs began to salivate when they heard the sound. Eventually, he was able to show that, even if there was no food around and he pressed the buzzer, the dogs would still salivate. The pairing of the buzzer with the anticipation of the food had caused an involuntary salivation response. This phenomenon is known as classical conditioning.

Behaviourists who study how animals learn use objective, standardised world-wide recognised terminology to explain the various components of classical conditioning (conditioning, by the way, is nothing more than a fancy term for learning).

Learn the lingo!

So let's go through Pavlov's experiment again – but this time with the recognised terms of classical conditioning:

This is what happened when Pavlov first started the experiment:

- The conditioned stimulus (the CS) = the buzzer (a meaningless or neutral 'thing' which the dog learnt to associate with something significant).
- The unconditioned stimulus (the UCS) = the food (something of importance which the dog did not need to learn about; in this case the food).
- The unconditioned response (the UCR) = the salivation (an unlearned or involuntary response to the UCS, the food).

Then . . .

- After Pavlov had repeated the experiment many times, when the buzzer was pressed the UCR changed to an automatic, involuntary response.
- The conditioned response (CR) = still the salivation, but the dogs had learnt to associate the CS with the UCS.

With Pavlov's dogs, the salivation happened because the dogs associated the sound of the buzzer with the pleasurable anticipation of food, but in classical conditioning, if something bad was to follow instead, we always refer to the animal's resultant behaviour as a Conditioned Emotional Response or CER. And this is where Inky comes in.

Powerful emotions

Think about the sorts of things that cause us humans to form powerful associations, the ones that make us have a Conditioned Emotional Response.

I have deliberately chosen examples that, hopefully, most of you will be able to relate to because, one of the most important things to understand about classical conditioning is that it is a very powerful type of learning – think about the bad food. No matter how irrational it may seem, how statistically unlikely it is that you would have another bad meal at the same restaurant, you have learned in such a powerful way that the food was extremely bad for you that it is very difficult to overturn or reverse that learning and you will probably never visit the same restaurant again.

This is exactly what had happened to Inky; she had formed a Conditioned Emotional Response to the field in a way that was just as powerful to her as food poisoning would be to you. And the more intense or traumatic the experience, the quicker the animal or person learns about it – sometimes just a one-off incident is enough for the association to remain embedded in the brain forever. So imagine how you would feel if you were asked to eat the same food again that had poisoned you and then you begin to have an understanding why leaving Inky in the field was such inappropriate advice for Angela!

Here are some examples of stimuli:

Conditioned stimulus	Smell in dentist surgery
Unconditioned stimulus	Fear or anxiety
Conditioned Emotional Response	Sweaty palms, or 'butterflies' in your tummy

Or:

Conditioned stimulus	Bad food (the sort that would give you food poisoning)
Unconditioned stimulus	Feelings of nausea
Conditioned Emotional Response	Vomiting

Solutions for Inky

In Inky's case the actual behavioural modification programme was relatively easy to select (see Chapter 16 for a detailed analysis of how I approach behaviour problems):

1. Give her a choice between stable and field

I wanted Inky to have constant access to her stable and field so that she would have a choice that did not involve her being forced to remain in the field. The design of Angela's yard was helpfully convenient and so we left the field gate open and allowed Inky permanent free movement between the stable, along the joining track and into the field. It was not important in the early stages of the programme if Inky spent the majority of the time in her stable – this was, after all, where she felt safest and the CER to the field was very powerful.

2. Build her trust in people

Whilst this was going on, I devised a programme for Angela which was designed to help build Inky's trust in people, and Angela in particular. The programme was put together after Angela completed an extensive questionnaire in which she was asked to rank many of Inky's behaviours by scoring them out of 10. By collating Inky's high and low scores, it was possible to deduce that, in fact, Inky had very little touch acceptance of people, let alone being handled or caught by people!

Positive Horse Magic for touch acceptance

Touch acceptance in horses is an idea I have borrowed from dolphin trainers. Dolphins trained in captivity are subject to strict welfare laws to ensure their wellbeing, and they have regular blood tests to check the stress hormone levels as I described above. But dolphins have an unusual response to stress – they withhold their blood – so stressed dolphins cannot easily be blood tested! The solution has been to train dolphins to a very high level of touch acceptance from humans so that, ultimately, the prick of a needle is of no concern to them.

In my dealings with problem horses, I often find that touch acceptance by the horse is very low, or only partial – the horse tolerating only certain parts of the body being touched. Improving acceptance is not something, in my view, that should be improved with the use of negative reinforcement. Angela had already been

dramatic change in Inky and an improvement in her anxiety. Inky started to voluntarily follow Jerry down the track to the field and, because she was not shut in behind the gate, she learnt to relax out there.

When I visited Inky on a follow-up visit, I was thrilled to see her grazing quietly in the field, and allowing Angela to catch her and lead on the track. Most times however, Angela simply allowed Inky to follow Jerry along the track and so, in the early stages, we kept the possible anxiety of being caught to the minimum. In a short space of time, Inky was well on her way to a total recovery and experiencing the pleasure of a close, trusting relationship with Angela.

It wasn't long before Inky was following Jerry along the track and relaxing in the field.

following our Positive Horse Magic series in *Horse&Rider* magazine and was interested in the use of positive reinforcement in the training of horses. We had a quick session to get Angela comfortable with using a clicker and how to 'click + treat' to let Inky know that a particular behaviour that she wanted was good. Inky really had only one behaviour that I was looking for her: relaxed calmness. As Angela worked her way through teaching Inky to being accepting of touch all over her body (later, to being groomed), each time Inky relaxed, Angela clicked + treated.

The combination of freedom to move around the yard, plus the touch acceptance programme were the two fundamental keys to improving Inky's agitation. Within days, Angela reported a

That's not all . . .

A surprise off-shoot to Inky's story lies in the fact that Angela had come to realise that maybe Jerry needed some attention, too. Although Jerry was, in many respects, the dream horse, because of my detailed analysis of Inky's behaviour, Angela knew that there was some things that Jerry was not entirely accepting of either (such as when he snaps the air when his girth is being tightened). Angela decided to attend a Positive Horse Magic course at the Natural Animal Centre and started to work with Jerry on the ground, doing things at liberty with him that she had not experienced ever before. She even decided that by using positive reinforcement training she could dispense with the bit when she rode Jerry in her school at home. Angela had come to realise that Jerry had not ever been fully accepting of the bit and that a more gentle, lateral approach in the form of a bitless hackamore, was needed.

In the end, the results in both Inky and Jerry were positive proof for Angela that a scientific approach to assessing behaviour and positive reinforcement training really works.

*Please note! In accordance with British law, Heather Simpson treats horses with behavioural problems only under referral from the owner's veterinary surgeon.

After her experience with Inky, Angela dedicated some time to Jerry, with positive results.

CHAPTER FOURTEEN

RUG REHAB!

After reading this chapter, you should be able to answer questions on the following:

■ That classical conditioning does not always involve just one stimulus
■ The biological notion of preparedness
■ Why, in this case, the horse associated his rug with fear
■ How to help a horse that is frightened of wearing a rug
■ How long solving the problem can take

In this chapter I will look at a second case of classical conditioning, where a horse forms a powerful association between an event and his response to it.

In this case, a frightening event occurred whilst the horse was in the field, just like the mare in the previous chapter. But this time, instead of the horse becoming fearful of the field only, he became fearful of the New Zealand rug he was wearing at the time as well. This combination of field + rug triggered such intense fear in the horse that the anxiety and worry over her horse's behaviour was becoming almost equally traumatic for his owner.

Tracey Hannan was almost at the point of

Ben – scared of his rug.

believing that no one could help her horse before she called the Natural Animal Centre. But once she understood the theory of what had happened to her horse – that is, the science of her horse's behaviour – she could relate to what had happened to him and realised that not only was a solution possible, but by working through a programme of behaviour modification, together we could put him back on the road to recovery.

A CARING OWNER

Tracey would do anything to keep her horses contented. Ben is a 12-year-old Warmblood gelding whom she had owned for nearly seven years. Tracey believed that he had always been a very easy-going horse but when Ben became terrified of his New Zealand rug, Tracey learnt that no amount of love and attention was enough to calm her horse down. When he wore his rug, it was as though a great wall of glass appeared between her and Ben – she was not able to get through to him and, in his terror, he was unable to react positively to her, either.

Tracey called me out to visit Ben in the autumn but in actual fact, his fear of rugs had started the year before. As the nights drew in and the days got colder, Tracey started to realise that what had been a problem the previous winter was about to become even worse. She knew she needed to get help as quickly as possible. Furthermore, in this particular year not only was Ben still scared of his rug, he had also become so difficult to lead from the field that a couple of times Tracey had been obliged to call out the vet to sedate him so that he could be led back to his stable.

Tracey also knew that other aspects of Ben's life were being affected; where the horse had previously been laid back about most of his handling and riding, she noticed that he was now much more nervous about being schooled or lunged. It seemed that the fear of his rug was having a knock-on effect on many other things and, clearly, this state of affairs could not continue.

Extreme terror

Ben's fear of his rug was not a mild emotion; we are talking about a horse whose every muscle in his body suggested extreme terror. He trembled and sweated and, if he was put out in the field, would spend a large amount of time either shaking at the gate or frozen under a particular tree. He was so scared of the rug that he was too frightened even to walk whilst he was wearing it.

Although I am aware that some people might think that the solution to Ben's problem would be to flood him and leave him out in the field with the rug on until he stopped showing the behaviour, only the most hard-hearted of trainers could have gone down this road had they been faced with Ben's terror in person. At the consultation, it transpired that Ben had always been relaxed in the field and would wear his New Zealand rug without a problem until, one day, some building work was carried out in the field adjacent to Ben's. Although she had not realised the significance at the time, Tracey remembered that Ben had been very upset that day. Just one afternoon of large construction vehicles roaring up and down had been enough for Ben to form the very powerful association between the field, his rug and his fear.

Irrational you might think? Well, possibly, but let's go back to my food poisoning example. Let's assume you always go to the same pizza parlour every week. Suddenly one evening, after your meal, you come down with food poisoning. Chances are, you will never go back to that restaurant again even though, from a rational point of view, the probability of you being poisoned again are very remote. You would disregard all the experiences you had when you were not ill and focus only on the one event which was traumatic. Remember, if the association between two things is particularly intense, then the trigger for the same emotion or response perpetuates, no matter how irrational it seems.

Bio-logical!

In an experiment where quails were made nauseous by being offered sour water, the quails did not make the association between feeling sick and the water until the researchers coloured the water with a blue dye. Suddenly, the quails did make the association and they avoided the water even when they were thirsty.

After working through a well though-out programme, Tracey was able to reintroduce Ben to his New Zealand rug.

101

Interestingly, the association was so powerful for these quails that they began to avoid all things blue in the environment as well, and researchers have suggested that because quails are attracted to different colours as potential food sources, they are biologically programmed to be more ready or prepared to accept colour as something potentially life threatening, too.

Similarly Ben, as a horse, was also prepared to view large, noisy, unfamiliar objects as life threatening and, just like the quails who thought it was the colour blue that made them sick, Ben associated the rug with his terror. Going back to my pizza example, it might be possible to prove to you that it was actually only the cheese that made you ill, but you would probably be unconvinced and remain steadfast in your avoidance of pizzas altogether.

Teaching Ben to accept his rug

It was crucial to success that we unravelled the association of fear with the rug in Ben's mind (See Chapter 16 for more detail of how to assess horse behaviour problems). Exactly like Angela McCrickard in Chapter 13, Tracey had also been reading the monthly series on Positive Horse Magic in *Horse&Rider* magazine, but had not yet tried using the clicker. I wanted to use the clicker as a marker for good behaviour in Ben – that is, being calm when wearing a rug – and then reward him with a treat. But Ben was not going to offer us that calmness in his present condition. So we had to go through the following steps:

Step 1 Teach Ben what the clicker meant so that he built up a positive association between click + treat and calm behaviour when he was not wearing a rug.

Step 2 Tracey practised clicker training with Ben around the stable area, in her school, and doing things like leading him to and from the field – all without the rug.

Step 3 When Ben understood what was required, we introduced a small cloth. If he would accept just a tiny cloth, the size of a tea towel on his back, then we would positively reinforce him with food.

Step 4 Gradually, over a few weeks as Ben was ready, we introduced bigger cloths, towels and, eventually, a light-weight summer sheet. Again, Tracey practised having Ben wear all these items calmly in the yard, the school and the field.

Step 5 Tracey was now able to re-introduce the New Zealand rug to Ben. He learnt to wear it in his stable, around the yard and even to load into a trailer whilst wearing it. Little by little, she was able to start leading him away from his stable towards the field and even achieve her ultimate goal, have him wear the rug in the field once again*.

*Note: at no time was Ben left alone in the field with his New Zealand rug during this process. This would have set back the programme and could even have made his fear more intense. A typical rate of improvement in a problem such as this depends, to some extent, on the temperament of the horse and the time the owner can invest. Resolution can be anything between one and eight weeks, based on 15 minutes practice per day. Obviously, if you are able to do one or two more sessions in a day, then the rate of improvement increases.

The essence of successful counter-conditioning is time – and Tracey gave Ben all that he needed to feel relaxed again with his rug.

At last Ben was no longer afraid of his New Zealand rug!

CHAPTER FIFTEEN

EDUCATING A HORSE HOUDINI!

After reading this chapter, you should be able to answer questions on the following:

- What a compound stimulus is
- The possible causes of agoraphobia in a horse
- How to analyse the classical conditioning, in this case using scientific learning theory terminology
- Why the need to find a pair-bond for the horse was part of the behavioural modification
- How to use play and positive reinforcement to teach a horse to lead safely

Imagine a 17hh Suffolk-Punch-cross cantering at full speed along your road – and then think about stepping out to stop him! Well, that's what the good folk of Jersey, Channel Islands had to get used to. Kismet, a 12-year-old gelding, had escaped so many times from his field that his previous owners had resorted to parking a JCB in front of his stable to keep him inside! This was all due to the fact that Kismet almost caused an accident with a passing motorist. Jersey police said that Kismet had been dangerously out of control on a public thoroughfare, so Kismet was condemned to life in a stable. Not a good outlook for any horse, let alone one of Kismet's size.

Quality of life

Debbie de Sainte Croix had known Kismet for

Heather soon realised that Kismit wasn't as confident as he appeared.

years and as the Equine Manager at the Quality of Life Sanctuary in Jersey, had often been called out by the police to help catch this equine escape artist. And it was when Debbie started studying for the Equine Behaviour Qualification (EBQ) at the Natural Animal Centre that she told me about Kismet.

Says Debbie: "Once I started to learn more about horse behaviour on the EBQ, I realised that Ross and Heather were probably the only people who knew how to help Kismet. Conventional training methods don't address things like trying to handle a habitual escaper!

"One trainer had tried to chase Kismet around a round pen, but this had only made him try to escape even more. Others had tried various negative reinforcement techniques and none had worked. What's more, when Kismet got excited, he became very bargy, he would walk right through you – and being the size he is, he is actually quite dangerous."

In the beginning

Kismet arrived at the Natural Animal Centre one April and, because he'd had a long journey on the ferry, I wanted him to stretch his legs in the arena. Nevertheless, the whole team was on stand-by just in case Kismet decided to do a disappearing act! But, in spite of his reputation, when I saw Kismet for the first time I realised that I had a very unconfident horse on my hands. He had not taken water since the previous day and was initially too nervous to lower his head into the bucket, a sure sign that he was feeling unsafe and extra-vigilant in his new surroundings.

My own horses were grazing in a field 10 acres away but even though Kismet had a good view of them from the arena, he showed no interest at all. Most horses that visit the Centre will stare fixedly at the herd, or even attempt to call the herd's attention to themselves by vocalizing loudly, but Kismet showed none of these signs and I soon realised that I was dealing with a horse who placed little reliance on other horses.

This can happen if the horse has been denied opportunities to interact and play with other horses during the first six months of its life, an important phase in the development of the young horse. However, it was equally likely that, in Kismet's case, he had learnt to get along as best as he could in life without equine companionship because he had spent so much

of his adult life in a stable. He had learnt to simply shut out the presence of other horses.

Kismet meets Troy

The obvious goal was to make Kismet feel comfortable enough in a field so that he would not think of escaping. My scientific knowledge told me that this was unlikely to happen unless I could get Kismet to accept – and ultimately rely on – equine companionship. Without a horse in his field, there was always the possibility that Kismet would be motivated to jump out even though, at this early stage, I had not yet found out what that motivation was. So I started by introducing Kismet to the Natural Animal Centre's, Troy, an old hand at meeting new horses and the most benign of individuals who seldom uses aggressive communication signals. In fact, Troy is so secure in the herd that he demonstrates his friendliness by grooming a

When Kismet met Troy. It was Troy's job to befriend Kismet to get used to other horses – a job he has experience in!

Aim of the game

Next, we successfully introduced Troy's pair-bond, Panda, to Kismet and then we led him to the field next to where the main herd was grazing. The aim was to keep him alongside other horses to encourage his interest in them. Although letting him loose into the field meant that Kismet might try escaping, because of the layout of the Natural Animal Centre, I knew he could not get far. But what Kismet did next was very revealing. Loose in the field, he showed signs of panic. He cantered along the fence line and only when he found the gate did he jump out. In other words, although he could easily have cleared the fence at any point, it was only at the gate that he jumped.

Oddly, but backing up my assessment of his lack of reliance on other horses, Kismet jumped the gate farthest away from the herd. Most horses jump a gate *towards* the safety of others, but Kismet's fear of the field was so great that escaping back to the yard was his only thought. So, something akin to agoraphobia was the driving motivation for Kismet's behaviour. It may seem strange to think that horses – open plains animals – could suffer from fear of open spaces but this was, indeed, at the root of Kismet's problems. But Kismet was also an escaper from stables so, clearly, very small spaces did not make him comfortable, either. In fact, later we were to discover that the space of our barn was about perfect as far as Kismet was concerned – neither too big nor too small.

The classical conditioning

Why Kismet was agoraphobic is, to some extent, open to speculation – too much time spent in a stable is the likeliest cause. However, from a scientific perspective he was showing a Conditioned Emotional Response and an analysis of his classically conditioning looked like this:

Conditioned stimulus = field + fence + gate (because there are three stimuli chained together, we call this a compound stimulus)
paired with
Unconditioned stimulus = agoraphobia or feelings of terror
leads to:
Conditioned Emotional Response = jumping the gate.

new arrival within a matter of minutes.

Troy came to the arena gate, started sniffing Kismet and, true to form, soon began grooming him. Troy was then let into the arena and the pair wandered around happily together. Then, finally, Kismet had a drink, a good sign that using another horse as part of the rehabilitation was going to work.

Whilst the horses got used to each other, I talked to one of Debbie's staff who knew Kismet well.

She told me: "Everyone who thinks they know Kismet says he's evil, that he needs a bullet or to be taught a lesson. Although he's big, he is very sensitive. I know he has potential but I feel he is NOT happy and it upsets me. He's been branded *The Devil Horse* which he is not at all."

Clearly, many people had completely misunderstood the motivation for Kismet's behaviour!

Because Kismet had shown it was the gate, not the fence, that was the trigger for jumping out, by simply opening the gate, his escaping would stop. I presumed that previously when Kismet jumped a gate and landed in another field, he would have jumped the gate in this field too and would, in theory, have kept going until he ran out of gates. By this time his panic would have been so entrenched that he was extremely difficult to stop, as Debbie had testified.

So we opened all the gates and, by removing the gate trigger out of the equation, I surmised that Kismet would not act out the escape behaviour . . . and that is exactly what happened. He continued to run around initially, and would rush through gateways, but in a very short space of time he learnt that whenever he passed through one gateway, he was not trapped and that there was always another for him to 'escape' through. Then Kismet discovered he could just walk through the gate and all the puff came out of his panic and he began to calm down.

So now an analysis of his classical conditioning looked like this:

Conditioned stimulus = field + fence + opened gap
paired with
Unconditioned stimulus = reducing anxiety
leads to:
Conditioned Response = walking through gateway.

A friend for life

Obviously, Kismet could not be left forever in an environment where all the gates were left open, but in those first few days, Kismet had as much space as he wanted at the Natural Animal Centre and, as a result, there were no escape attempts. After three days we were able to shut the gate to his field – without him even noticing. He had his head down and just kept on grazing!

As I mentioned earlier, my goal was to get Kismet contented in a field with an equine companion. Even though he was not trying to

It was some time before Kismet could relax with a fence!

The new Kismet with his pair-bond Gemma – a crucial part of Kismet's rehabilitation process of feeling safe in a field.

escape, I knew his confidence was fragile and the slightest change – either within his field or the one where my horses were – could be enough to trigger his fear again.

I also wanted Kismet to enjoy time out in the field in the sunshine with ample grazing, and as the weeks went by and he began to enjoy life once again, Kismet also gradually began to show an interest in my horses, and even nuzzle some of them over the fence. Now was the time to introduce him to a new companion. You read in Chapter One that it is not only an important need of the horse that he lives in a herd, but also that he be allowed to form a pair-bond. This means having someone special to play with, to groom you and, of course, to watch out for you – particularly while you sleep.

There was no point in letting Kismet form a special bond with one of our horses as he was only a temporary visitor and the whole basis of the behaviour modification was that, when he left us, he would not revert to escaping again. The way forward was to get him comfortable with an equine companion who would remain with him for the long-term and, most importantly, would help him retain the feelings of being safe and calm.

Special visitor

When Debbie returned to us to pursue her EBQ studies a month later, she enthusiastically embraced the idea.

"When I saw Kismet then, he looked so happy. I had never seen him grooming another horse before. Even at the Sanctuary he had always seemed too frightened."

After a few day's consultation back in Jersey, Debbie rang me to say that she had found a likely companion for Kismet. Within the week Gemma had arrived, a 14-year-old mare, who had been living at the Quality of Life sanctuary for the past three years. It took Kismet a few days to settle with his new companion but within a couple of weeks they had become firm friends. Sceptics might be tempted to say that we were setting up a future problem for ourselves that was likely to end in separation anxiety for one or both of the horses. To such people, I say, "One step at a time!" Separation anxiety does not occur where a horse is confident that his companion will always return – it is a symptom of lack of confidence and a sense of abandonment, both factors which were being addressed in Kismet's overall therapy.

Clicker training with Positive Horse Magic helped Kismet to realise that he could have fun – without scaring his human friends.

POSITIVE HORSE MAGIC

In terms of re-commencing his training, I believed that the only way forward for Kismet was positive reinforcement, the basis of the Positive Horse Magic training system. Because Kismet was also a barger and difficult to lead, teaching him to listen for the clicker was crucial. Helping him learn to slow down when he felt panicky was the key because barging was just another example of his fear (certainly not disrespect, as some people had told Debbie). From this point, teaching him to lead was really easy.

A few months later, Debbie came to spend the day with Kismet to see how he was getting on. She had this to say;

"I had seen dogs trained with positive reinforcement and was amazed at how quickly they learnt, but I had never seen it done with horses. I came prepared to see something different being done with Kismet but what I saw today was beyond my wildest expectations. It's no exaggeration to say that Heather has saved Kismet's life. To see him running around playing with the ball and looking so happy makes me want to cry with joy for him. At last, this horse is learning to be a horse!"

CHAPTER SIXTEEN

THE NATURAL ANIMAL CENTRE BEHAVIOUR TRIANGLE

After reading this chapter, you should be able to answer questions on the following:

- How the Natural Animal Centre's Behavioural Triangle works
- The importance of cognitive therapy in solving horse behaviour problems
- How the Behavioural Triangle and cognitive therapy work together in parallel
- How to solve a simple horse behaviour problem (biting when being girthed up) using both approaches

At the Natural Animal Centre, Ross and I see a huge range of behavioural problems that people are experiencing with their horses. But from the most serious case, say of self-mutilation, to the more mundane of training problems, leading a horse safely from A to B, for example, there is almost always a common thread in people's approaches to fixing the problems. Generally, they are unaware of the priorities of the horse's behavioural needs and, because they do not take account of these, problem solving can be laborious and even traumatic for the horse.

In Chapter Three I explained that the horse continually has a number of behavioural choices in his life – should he eat now or should he rest, instead? Should he challenge a higher-ranking horse, or not? But it is also important for us to know that when the horse is under some form of pressure and showing a behaviour problem, we might say that he reverts to the same priority of choices – that fixed list which has evolved over millions of years and is designed to enhance his fitness for both survival and reproduction.

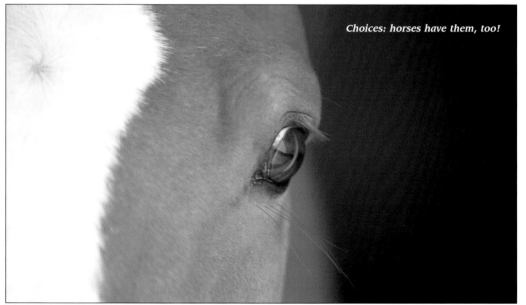

Choices: horses have them, too!

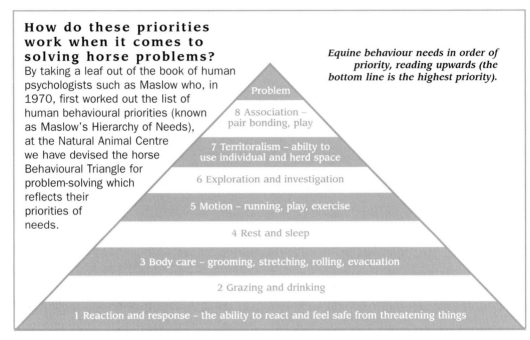

How do these priorities work when it comes to solving horse problems?

By taking a leaf out of the book of human psychologists such as Maslow who, in 1970, first worked out the list of human behavioural priorities (known as Maslow's Hierarchy of Needs), at the Natural Animal Centre we have devised the horse Behavioural Triangle for problem-solving which reflects their priorities of needs.

Equine behaviour needs in order of priority, reading upwards (the bottom line is the highest priority).

Problem

8 Association – pair bonding, play

7 Territoralism – abilty to use individual and herd space

6 Exploration and investigation

5 Motion – running, play, exercise

4 Rest and sleep

3 Body care – grooming, stretching, rolling, evacuation

2 Grazing and drinking

1 Reaction and response – the ability to react and feel safe from threatening things

A cognitive approach

The priority of horse behaviours is not the only approach I rely on when helping horses with problems. I also use a strategy used in human psychotherapy – cognitive therapy – but of course, adapted appropriately for equine needs.

Cognitive therapy is a technique that was originally formulated by Aaron Beck, a psychiatrist who worked with depressed patients. He noticed that depressed people often made what he called *cognitive distortions* that is, they interpreted events in a very negative and pessimistic way, even though these events may not have warranted such a bleak assessment.

Beck also said that classical conditioning played an important role in the entrenching of these distorted emotions. For example, he thought that the combination of 'conditioned thoughts' (CS) + 'feelings/emotions' (the UCS) led to the behaviour of depression. So somebody who was suffering from depression as a result of an unhappy work situation, might show the following pattern when they first got up in the morning:

CS	=	[thoughts of] the workplace
UCS	=	[emotions of] pessimism
CER	=	lowering of mood (ie become even more depressed).

In trying to find a solution using cognitive therapy, you do not need to focus on the depressed behaviour (the CER). Rather, you would focus on the emotions and thoughts of the patient and, in particular, when the patient paired these two together.

So in the above example, for instance, cognitive therapy might include:

CS = [thoughts of] the workplace + fun task/puzzle
UCS = [emotions of] increased self esteem [because patient is able to do puzzle]
CER = lifting of mood to more positive things

So what do I take out of cognitive therapy techniques when it comes to solving horse behaviour problems at the Natural Animal Centre? Two elements key to both cognitive therapy and horse problem-solving are that both incorporate:
- A step-by-step process.
- Conditioned reinforcement – that is, the learning theory of classical conditioning and instrumental learning using positive reinforcement.

So in horse behaviour modification, we try to change the horse's emotions with respect to certain stimuli. Can I change this horse's thoughts and emotions about grinding on a bit, or bolting down a bridlepath? This is the opposite of what most current horse trainers do because they tend to focus only on the CER.

The bottom line in cognitive therapy is that a CS paired with a UCS will give a certain behaviour, and if I only look at the behaviour and ignore the UCS, I am pretty much doomed to fail or, at best, only get the horse to put a lid on the unwanted behaviour for just a while.

The Behavioural Triangle and cognitive therapy – a parallel approach

Because horses place such a high priority on being safe (ie the behaviour at the base of the Behaviour Triangle), my focus in a behaviour consultation is (through cognitive therapy techniques) to keep pairing this feeling of safety (ie the UCS) with all the things in the environment that are causing the exact opposite, troubling emotions in the horse. And, little by little, the horse learns to change his attitude towards the problem, not just temporarily but permanently – and all because of the power of classical conditioning.

Solving a typical problem: biting when being girthed

Let's look at the Behaviour Triangle in a little more detail with a typical behavioural problem: an owner calls the Natural Animal Centre – she cannot girth up her horse without being bitten.

At a behaviour consultation, instead of immediately leaping in trying to fix the girthing problem (the top of the Triangle), I start at the bottom of the Triangle and find out first which of the horse's needs are being met. I would explain to the owner that if the needs lower down the Triangle have not been met, then she has, at best, an upward struggle in trying to solve the behaviour at the top of the heap – the straw that broke the camel's back, if you like. The straw, or girth in this case, is often just a symptom of a lot more that is going on in the horse's life which is causing him unhappiness.

At a consultation, I would learn from the owner that there are other issues involved also – for example:

- She has trouble catching the horse in the field.
- The horse evades the saddle by dipping its back (there are no pain or discomfort reasons for this – the horse has already been checked out for back pain or poorly fitting saddle).
- He is nappy when out hacking.

I would explain to the owner that the horse's safety needs right at the bottom of the triangle have not been met:

- Because he is so closely bonded to his pair-bond, he does not want to be separated from his friend and so runs away when she tries to catch him.
- He is actually frightened of the saddle because he has never been properly introduced to it.
- Through previous learning experiences, he now associates the girth with emotions like fear and pain.
- By asking him to cope with being tacked up and then ridden without his pair-bond at his side is too big a leap from the bottom to the top of the triangle. The horse tries to show that his ability to cope is breaking down by biting and then napping when the rider is on board. Napping is a display both of fear of being alone and fear of exploring new places.

Step one: target an object - positive reinforcement.

Step two: with pair-bond Dream, Bjorn gains confidence.

Here, with Ross as demonstrator and using Natural Animal Centre's horses Bjorn and Dream, you can see how I would devise a strategy to cure the problem:

1. Using positive reinforcement only (that is, giving the horse a click and a treat for the behaviour he wants), Ross starts off by teaching Bjorn to touch a target object, in this case a white cloth.

2. He has brought Dream into the arena also, thus taking care of one of Bjorn's important safety needs – having an equine friend at his side whilst he learns new things.

3. Ross then teaches Bjorn to touch the end of a target stick, again rewarding the horse for every touch he makes.

4. He asks Bjorn to follow the target stick, thereby introducing movement into the equation, but all done without force. (You can develop these targeting skills in trot and eventually canter, teaching your horse to circle around you and the target stick).

5. Ross now progresses to things like asking Bjorn to jump over a barrel.

6. Bjorn next targets onto the saddle and Ross clicks and treats him for touching it on the fence.

7. Gradually, Ross moves to placing the saddle gently on Bjorn's back – he is not even thinking about introducing the girth at this stage.

8. Once Bjorn can walk around with the saddle on his back, doing up the girth can be introduced – Ross clicks and treats for Bjorn's calmness (his emotion of feeling safe – the behaviour at the base of the Triangle) as he raises the girth centimetre by centimetre.

9. Now Bjorn is ready for a real 'safety-check' – how safe does he feel when he is asked to go into trailer? Note, Dream is still allowed to observe the proceeding, thus giving Bjorn a sense of equine solidarity! We know that Dream is safe loose because she is pair-bonded with Bjorn and because both horses are calm.

10. Now Bjorn is ready to ride! Still using positive reinforcement, Ross asks Bjorn to follow the target stick, exactly as he had done previously without a rider on his back. Ross practises asking Bjorn to follow the stick to both the left and the right. By this stage, the target stick in itself has become a symbol for safety and calmness – the mere sight of it is enough to induce calmness in Bjorn. The element of classical conditioning is then achieved by repeating the process several times.

11. Ross then asks Bjorn to move from one cone to another and clicks and treats him for touching each one. What Ross is actually doing is reinforcing calmness and relaxation in Bjorn, as well as training the halt! The two are virtually indistinguishable at this stage.

12. Ross develops Bjorn's feelings of safety by trying different manoeuvres in the arena, and once again jumps Bjorn over a barrel – but this time, with himself on board.

13. Ross keeps checking Bjorn's level of responsiveness – if he gets too excited jumping over a barrel, he asks Bjorn to touch the white cloth on the other side of the jump.

Step three: with the target stick, still rewarding.

Step four: over the jump!

14. Bjorn practises new manoeuvres like 20m circles and spirals – Ross is now chaining together a number of steps before he clicks and treats Bjorn for doing well.

By this stage, the objective of the Behavioural Triangle approach will have been achieved and the horse's attitude towards the girth will have altered permanently and in a positive way.

Step five: the saddle is now the target.

Step six: click and treat for remaining calm.

Step eight: now saddled, it's back to a familiar movement; jumping the barrel, with a rider on board.

Step seven: confidence testing; Bjorn is happy to go into the trailer.

10 POINT PLAN FOR PROBLEM-SOLVING

GIVE YOURSELF THE BEST CHANCE OF SOLVING EQUINE BEHAVIOUR PROBLEMS BY REMEMBERING 10 VITAL POINTS

After reading this chapter, you should be able to answer questions on the following:

- Why a structured approach to problem-solving is necessary
- The four reinforcers, and why positive reinforcement in particular is helpful in problem-solving
- The meaning of habituation
- The value of being able to recognise automatic behaviours
- The value of clicker training in problem-solving
- The importance of being educated in the behaviour of horses
- Good management as part of the solution
- Why early traumatic experiences play a role in the development of problems
- The importance of having a time scale in problem-solving
- The value of positive support from people around you
- How to choose a professional trainer

I do not know how to fly an aeroplane and if I were asked to help out with a plane that was showing problems whilst already in the air, I know I would be overwhelmed by all the equipment and it would be unlikely that I would be able to solve anything.

But so many people – no more equipped to deal with finding solutions for horse behaviour problems than I am for aeroplane problem-solving – find themselves not only trying to sort out the problems, but feeling very disappointed with themselves when things do not work out.

Some of my work involves helping people with their horse on a one-to-one basis. A consultation usually lasts about an hour and people often ask me how I manage to assess the horse, prioritise in my mind which problems I am going to tackle, explain all this to the owner and, finally, run through a behaviour plan for her to work through, so quickly.

There is a wealth of animal behavioural research which concentrates on solving problem behaviour in animals, and there is nothing special about being able to run an animal behavioural consultation – once you have had the training and know what to look for. However,

Ross asks Bjorn to circle at trot following a target stick . . .

. . . he then reinforces Bjorn with a click and a treat.

A structured approach

This is the sort of list that I have in my mind when I am running a horse behaviour consultation; without a structured approach to the problem, I would not be able to give an owner any meaningful assistance within a one-hour time-frame. Of course, it is not possible to turn you instantly into a behavioural scientist but if you are having problems with your horse, by running through this checklist of points before you even touch him, you already have a fighting chance of solving the issue. I am not trying to say that this list will let you fix any horse with any problem in just one hour. But without a list like this, you will most likely flounder from one technique to another in a haphazard way, and may eventually start to think that force is the only way forward. This list will help you plan what you need to do to help your horse, and give you a better chance of succeeding.

The first five points of the plan focus on your knowledge. Quite simply, without knowledge and information, you will not easily solve problems.

1. Understand the difference between the four reinforcers – nice or nasty?

■ **Positive reinforcement** – add something nice when your horse performs a wanted behaviour. Here Ross asks Bjorn to circle him at the trot by following a target stick. Ross then reinforces Bjorn with a click and a treat to let Bjorn know that he is pleased with him.

■ **Negative reinforcement** – take away something nasty when a horse performs a wanted behaviour eg, keep flicking a whip behind a horse until he circles around you; then you stop the flicking.

Remember: both positive and negative reinforcement always increase the likelihood of a behaviour happening.

■ **Positive Punishment** – add something nasty to get a horse to stop an unwanted behaviour, such as throwing a rope at a horse to stop him coming in when working in a round pen.

■ **Negative Punishment** – take away something nice to get a horse to stop an unwanted behaviour, such as taking the horse's food away when he kicks at the stable door.

Remember: both positive and negative punishment always decrease the likelihood of a behaviour happening.

Why do we need to concern ourselves with these reinforcers? After all, horse training has relied on negative reinforcement and positive punishment for hundreds of years! But behavioural scientists (famously, Skinner and many others who succeeded him) showed what the consequences of using the different reinforcers are on an animal.

In a scientific experiment, horses were divided into two groups but both were required to go through a maze. The first group received a mild electric shock when they took a wrong turn but the second group received a food reward when they took the correct turn.

The behavioural scientists proved that the horses which received the negative (or nasty) reinforcer, took much more time to solve the problem of getting through the maze. They also took longer and longer to make a decision when they reached a junction in the maze. This makes sense because the electric shock was a positive punisher. On the other hand, the positively reinforced group of horses got faster and faster at not only making a decision, but also the correct one – in other words they learnt faster and were better at problem-solving.

If we use positive reinforcement – that is, 'a click + reward' approach – not only does the problem-solving becoming less stressful for both horse and human, but the problem is likely to be resolved much quicker.

2. Understand habituation

When we try to teach a horse that something he considers frightening isn't really so, then we are in the area behaviourists call habituation.

I know that hosing down my horse's legs is not a life-threatening experience – but my horse, in the beginning, does not necessarily agree. If I push too hard and too quickly, instead of getting my horse used to something (ie habituating him to a hose), I might end up sensitising him instead (ie increasing the fear).

For successful habituation, horses need to be taught that certain things are not threatening in a variety of contexts. Here, Ross helps Jessica learn to have her feet picked out – a potentially threatening experience for a horse – by habituating her in the field, then in the school, then in the yard. Ross needs to keep changing

Habituation – same situation, difference places.

the context three or four times for habituation to picking out feet to be successful.

This is a critical point often missed in problem-solving. How often I hear people tell me that a horse can do something at home, but is not able to do it at a competition. This has happened because the owner has misunderstood habituation – but happily, it is easily resolved.

3. Understand conditioning

In Chapters 13 to 15, I presented you with three real-life cases where horses had become so conditioned to a problem that their fear had become automatic. For example, in one case, the horse Kismet was so frightened of being alone in his paddock, that he automatically jumped the gate when he was turned out.

Understanding conditioning is important and will affect the timescales of solving the problem (on page 122). Have your horse's responses to the problem become automatic? If they are, then they may have become more entrenched. But we still do not resort to force – in fact, in conditioned responses we are extra careful that the horse never shows fear when we are problem-solving as this might make matters worse. With Kismet, we only used positive reinforcement, clicker training and play to turn him from a frightened, withdrawn animal into an exuberant playmate and a joy to be around.

4. Understand the importance of the clicker in training

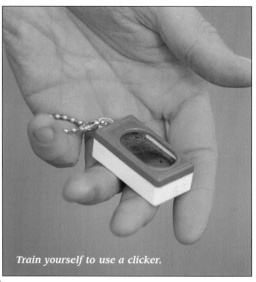

Train yourself to use a clicker.

Why do we at the Natural Animal Centre use the clicker as the pivot of all problem-solving? Because it is such an easy thing for the horse to learn! Quite simply, all you need to know is that the clicker is a marker (behaviourists call it a bridge) for reinforcing a behaviour you want – you click when your horse performs a desired behaviour and you pair that with a treat. Very soon your horse starts to think 'What do I need to do to get you to click?' and once you have him thinking like this, then both the horse and you are thinking about solving a problem – only clicker training gives you this exciting joint approach.

Not only is it nicer for both you and your horse to be working together on the problem, you avoid all the anxieties that are caused by using negative reinforcement. And it has been proven that using positive reinforcement is the fastest way of problem-solving!

5. Get really good at horse behaviour!

This is a bit like trying to pick your way through a minefield! When I teach the Equine Behaviour Qualification, I always start by asking,

Observation – a key method of learning horse behaviour.

"Where can horse owners go to get information about horse behaviour they can trust and rely upon?" There is so much mis-information but the reality is that there is plenty of scientific horse research going on across the world – so accurate information does exist.

Try not to follow the crowd when solving your horse's problem. Work out his individual needs. You know him better than anyone. Read as much as you can, go on a horse behaviour course and then pool all this information together in a way that works for your horse.

Horses may become closely bonded with another.

6. Evaluate how your horse is managed

No matter what problem your horse is suffering from, if he is inappropriately managed outside of the training or problem-solving sessions, then getting to a solution will take much longer (or in some cases, may never happen).

If your horse has become closely bonded with one of the other horses in the yard and shows separation anxiety whenever the pair-bond is removed, then the solution is not to maintain social isolation by stabling your horse for hours and hours on his own. Using the Behavioural Triangle explained in the Chapter 16, you will appreciate that separation anxiety is a reflection that your horse does not feel safe and unless the base of the Triangle – the base of safety – is fulfilled, then your chances of curing separation anxiety are very small. By allowing your horse to spend more time with his companion and by practising separations (initially, just short bouts, increasing gradually) in a controlled, methodical way, you are much more likely to achieve a long-term solution.

7. Consider any socialisation problems or early weaning issues

It is now so well-known in human psychology that children's early experiences affect their behaviours in adulthood that dozens of television soap operas base their storylines on this fact, knowing that the majority of the audience has no training in psychology. Yet even though this has been proven in animals also, in the horse world we tend to ignore what has happened to our horse in someone else's hands when, in fact, we should be paying lots of attention to this issue.

Let's say you have a nappy horse. If you have not already asked, do some work on the telephone before you rush out and confront the problem with spurs or a bigger bit. Nappy horses have often been subjected to an unnatural, abrupt weaning, leaving them forever traumatised when separated from horses – unless something is done to help them get over the experience. If you find out from a previous owner that he was one of these unfortunates, then help solve the problem by letting your horse spend lots of time with a stable, adult companion. Arrange to hack out with that horse, gradually building up your horse's behavioural triangle from a solid base of learning to feel safe in the world again.

8. Understand the timescales of the problem

Doctors call this the *prognosis* – how long is it going to take for the patient to get better? If you went to see your doctor because you were complaining of a sore throat, you would want a prognosis – will I get better in three days or will it take much longer, like two weeks?

You should try to come up with a prognosis yourself for your horse's problem. Without this crucial factor, your goal of a solution remains forever open-ended. Part of the reason why behavioural scientists become so good at problem-solving is that – like doctors – they become excellent at making an accurate prognosis. To do this, they ask themselves certain questions which they then use as their guides.

Things that would suggest a horse behaviour problem might get resolved fairly quickly are:
■ The problem has only just started.
■ It only happens occasionally.
■ When it does happen, it only lasts for a short period of time.

Take the problem where a horse does not like having his belly groomed. If the problem only started after he had suffered a skin problem (which the vet has now fixed) and the horse only snatches at you occasionally, presumably when there is an occasional re-emergence of sensitivity, then your chances of helping your horse relax when having his belly groomed is extremely good.

However, if he has always been unaccepting of belly grooming and he is now 15 years old, if the problem has got worse over the years (from just snapping at the air in the beginning, to now biting you), and if the problem is now being directed at other people or horses (for example, the horse might now nip an equine neighbour whilst you groom him), then the prognosis is likely to be poorer.

Being aware of the prognosis will help you set

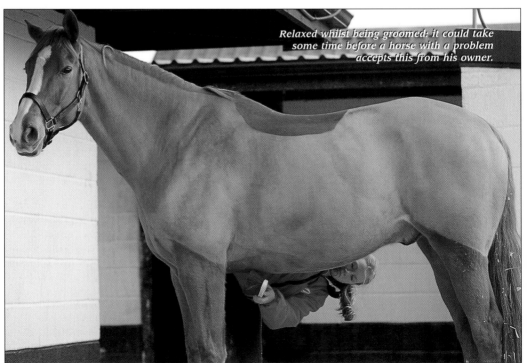

Relaxed whilst being groomed: it could take some time before a horse with a problem accepts this from his owner.

Positive support is important for you and your horse.

reasonable goals and will prevent you from placing unreasonable expectations on your horse. So many horses get sold on for behavioural reasons – because people expected an instant solution when the chances of that happening might have been, scientifically speaking, zero.

9. Surround yourself with people who will help you achieve your goals.

This might seem a small point but it is one of the biggest reasons I have seen people give up on a problem, and even give up on their horse. If you have your horse in a yard where everyone is an amateur expert, where everything good you try to do for your horse is criticised by others, then maybe it's time for you to be thinking about a change.

Surround yourself with people who are positive in their attitude towards each other and to each others' horses. Having to deal with a horse which is having problems is hard enough without having to take on a whole yard of criticism as well. Unfortunately, often using positive reinforcement techniques also attracts criticism. Generally, horse people are so unused to seeing positive techniques being used in horse training that they react with negativity. Don't let this kind of talk throw you off your path of trying to solve the problem without having to resort to force.

10. Decide whether to get a professional trainer involved

Perhaps by sitting down and working through this list you have decided that you really need to get a professional involved, after all. When you come to choose one, you should still use this list as a guide for selecting a trainer.

There are hundreds of horse trainers out there who, for example, do not know the difference between positive and negative reinforcement. If the trainer does not understand which technique he is employing, they could not possibly know what effect the technique is having on the horse's emotional wellbeing.

Ask lots of questions about the trainer's methods before you hire him, get references and find out if other people have been happy with his results with their horses.

By following the philosophical approach presented in this book, you will begin to realise that the idea of a 'quick fix' is rarely the way to go in solving behavioural problems in animals. Horses are beautiful, complicated creatures – and they deserve our patience and compassion.

A structured approach to problem-solving and the application of even the most basic equine behavioural science gives you an excellent chance of helping your horse through even more complex issues and paradoxically, like the proverbial hare and tortoise, this way gets you to your goal faster in the end.

To contact the Natural Animal Centre

Write: Natural Animal Centre
Penhill
Trawsmawr
Nr Carmarthen
Carmarthenshire
SA33 6ND

Tel: 0870 9913334
E-mail: natural@globalnet.co.uk
On the Web: www.naturalanimalcentre.com

REFERENCES

Rather than burden the reader with cumbersome references in the body of the text, and in the spirit of making this book read less like a scientific textbook and more like a practical guide, I have accumulated all references for further reading here, at the back of the book. The first section is a list of books and are therefore readily accessible to the horse owner. Some, however, are out of print, but are still well worth going the extra mile to locate.

It is true however, that 'real' science is sometimes only found in scientific journals and, although I have deemed these to be generally inappropriate for a book of this type (in terms of depth and level of scientific analysis), in the third reference section, you will find a number of the more well-known papers that are relevant to this book. For the reader who does indeed wish to study the original research, any librarian will point you in the right direction to locate these.

Section One Further reading in book form
1. Ball, S, Simpson, H and Howard, J (2001) *Emotional Healing for Horses*, C W Daniel & Co, Cambridge
2. Clutton Brock, J (1992) *Horse Power: a history of the horse and donkey in human societies*, Natural History Museum Publications, Great Britain
3. Dawkins, R (1976) *The Selfish Gene*, Oxford University Press, UK
4. De Grazia, D (1996) *Taking Animals Seriously, mental life and mental status*, Cambridge University Press, UK
5. Fiske, J (1979) *How Horses Learn*, Stephen Green, Vermont
6. Fraser, A (1992) *The Behaviour of the Horse*, CAB International, UK
7. Frey, R G (1983) *Rights, Killing and Suffering*, Blackwell Science, Oxford
8. Greenfield, S (2000) *The Private Life of the Brain*, Penguin, UK
9. Griffin, J (1992) *Animal Minds*, University of Chicago Press, USA
10. Groves, C P (1974) *Horses, Asses and Zebras in the Wild*, David & Charles, London
11. Holmes, J (1993) *John Bowlby and Attachment Theory*, Routledge, London
12. Kennedy, J S (1992) *The New Anthropomorphism*, Cambridge University Press, UK
13. Kiley-Worthington, M (1997) *The Behaviour of Horses in Relation to Management and Training*, J A Allen, London
14. Kiley-Worthington, M (1997) *Equine Welfare*, J A Allen, London
15. Loon, B (1996) *Introducing Darwin and Evolution*, Totem Books, USA
16. Manning, A and Stamp Dawkins, M (1993) *An Introduction to Animal Behaviour*, Cambridge University Press, UK
17. McDonnell, S (2003) – *A Practical Guide to Horse Behaviour: The Equid Ethogram*, Eclipse Press, USA
18. McGreevy, P (2000) *Why Does My Horse . . . ?*, Souvenir Press, UK
19. Mills, D and Nankervis, K (1999) *Equine Behaviour: Principles and Practice*, Blackwell Science, Oxford
20. Pryor, K (1985) *Don't Shoot the Dog! The new art of teaching and training*, Bantam Books, USA
21. Rees, L (1993) – *The Horse's Mind*, Stanley Paul Limited, UK
22. Robinson, I (ed) T*he Waltham Book of Human-animal Interaction: Benefits and Responsibilities of Pet Ownership*, Pergamon Press, UK

23. Rollin, B E (1981) *Animal Rights and Human Morality*, Prometheus, Buffalo
24. Rossdale, P D (2002) *The Horse from Conception to Maturity*, J A Allen, London
25. Schwartz, B, Wasserman, E & Robbins, S (2002) *Psychology of Learning and Behaviour*, W W Norton & Co, New York
26. Serpell, J (1996) *In the Company of Animals: a Study of Human-animal Relationships*, Cambridge University Press, UK
27. Sidman, M (2001) *Coercion and its Fallout*, Authors Cooperative Inc, Boston
28. Skinner, B F (1938) *The Behaviour of Organisms*, Appleton-Century, New York
29. Stamp Dawkins, M (1993) *Through Our Eyes Only: the Search for Animal Consciousness*, Spektrum Publishing, Germany
30. Waring, G (2003) *Horse Behaviour*, Noyes Publications, New York

Section Two DVDs, computer games and distance learning programmes
1. Bailey, B & Breland-Bailey, M, *Patient Like the Chipmunks* (video)
2. Karen Pryor, *Clicker Magic! The Art of Shaping* (video)
3. Ross and Heather Simpson, *Positive Horse Magic* (DVD)
4. Ross and Heather Simpson, *Positive Horse Magic Distance Learning Programme – a step-by-step guide to clicker training your horse at home*
5. Ross and Heather Simpson, information pack – *How to make your yard part of the Natural Animal Centre Approved Yard Scheme*
6. *Sniffy the Virtual Mouse*, for practising your learning theory and training skills on a software mouse (available through www.psychology.wadsworth.com/sniffy)

Section Three Further reading: papers in scientific journals and textbooks
1. Albiston, G & Brain, P F (1986) Adaption to unusual circumstances in feral ponies, *Applied Animal Behaviour Science*, 15, 87-88
2. Alloy, L B & Seligman, M E P (1979) On the cognitive components of learned helplessness and depression in Bower, G H (ed) *Psychology of learning and motivation*, 13, NY
3. Barber, J A & Crowell-Davis, S L (1994) Maternal behaviour of Belgian mares (Equus caballus), *Applied Animal Behaviour Science*, 41, 161-189
4. Barnard, C J & Hurst, J L (1996) Welfare by design: the natural selection of welfare criteria, *Animal Welfare*, 5, 405-433
5. Baum, W M (1970) Extinction of avoidance responses through prevention/flooding, *Psychological Bulletin*, 74, 276-284
6. Becker, C D & Ginsberg, J R (1990) Mother-infant behaviour of wild Grevy's zebra: adaptions for survival in semi-desert East Africa, *Animal Behaviour*, 40, 1111-1118
7. Bekoff, M & Byers J A (1998) *Animal play: evolutionary, comparative and ecological perspectives*, Cambridge University Press, UK
8. Berger, J (1977) Organizational systems and dominance in feral horses in the Grand Canyon, *Behavioural Ecology and Sociobiology*, 2, 131-146
9. Berger, J (1986) *Wild horses of the Great Basin: social*

competition and population size, University of Chicago Press, Chicago

10. Blackman, D (1977) Conditioned suppression and the effects of classical conditioning on operant behaviour in Honig, W K & Staddon (eds) *Handbook of operant behaviour*, Prentice-Hall, USA

11. Bolles, R C (1985) A cognitive, non-associative view of conditioned inhibition in Miller, R R & Spears N E (eds) *Information processing in animals: conditioned inhibition*, Erlbaum, USA

12. Bouton, M E & Bolles, R C (1979) Contextual control of the extinction of conditioned fear, *Learning and motivation*, 10, 445-466

13. Bowling, A T & Touchberry, R W (1990) Parentage of Great Basin feral horses, *Journal of Wildlife Management*, 54, 424-429

14. Boyd, L E (1988) Ontogeny of behaviour in Przewalski horses, *Applied Animal Behaviour Science*, 21, 41-69

15. Boyd, L E (1991) The Behaviour of Przewalski's horses and its importance to their management, *Applied Animal Behaviour Science*, 29, 301-318

16. Breland, K & Breland, M (1961) The misbehaviour of organisms, *American Psychologist*, 16, 681-684

17. Caanitz, H, O' Leary, L, Houpt, K, Petersson, K & Hintz H (1991) The effects of exercise on equine behaviour, *Applied Animal Behaviour Science*, 31, 1-12

18. Carlson, N R (1998) *Physiology of behaviour*, Allyn & Bacon, USA

19. Cautela, J R (1965) The problem of backward conditioning, *Journal of Psychology*, 60, 135-144

20. Chavatte, P (1991) Maternal behaviour in the horse: theory and practical applications to foal rejection and fostering, *Equine Veterinary Education*, 3, 215-220

21. Cheng, P W (1997) From covariation to causation: a causal power theory, *Psychological Review*, 104, 367-405

22. Colwill, R M (1993) An associative analysis of instrumental learning, *Current Directions in Psychological Science*, 2, 111-116

23. Colwill, R M & Rescorla, R A (1988) Associations between the discriminative stimulus and the reinforcer in instrumental learning, *Journal of Experimental Psychology: Animal Behaviour Processes*, 14, 155-164

24. Colwill, R M & Rescorla, R A (1990) Evidence for the hierarchical structure of instrumental learning, *Animal Learning and Behaviour*, 18, 71-82

25. Cooper, J J & Nicol, C J (1991) Stereotypies affect environmental preference in bank voles, *Animal Behaviour*, 41, 971-977

26. Cooper, J J & Nicol, C J (1993) The coping hypotheses of stereotypic behaviour: a reply to Rushen, *Animal Behaviour*, 45, 616-618

27. Cousins, M S, Atherton, A, Turner, L & Salamone, J D (1996) Nucleus accumbens dopamine depletions after relative response allocation in a T-maze cost-benefit task, *Behavioural Brain Research*, 74, 189-197

28. Crowell-Davis, S L (1986) Developmental behaviour in S L Crowell-Davis and K A Houpt (eds) *The Veterinary Clinics of North America, Equine Behaviour*, W B Saunders Co USA 573-590

29. Crowell-Davis, S L, Houpt, K A, Kane, L (1987) Play development in Welsh pony foals (Equus caballus), *Applied Animal Behaviour Science*, 18, 119-131

30. Dallaire, A & Ruckebusch, Y (1974) Sleep and wakefulness in the housed pony under different dietary conditions, *Canadian Journal of Medicine*, 38, 65-71

31. Denny, M R (91971) Relaxation theory and experiments in Brush, F R (ed) *Aversive conditioning and learning*, Academic Press, NY

32. Di Cara, L V (1970) Learning in the autonomic nervous system, *Scientific American*, 222, 30-39

33. Dinsmoor, J A (1983) Observing and conditioned reinforcement, *Behavioural and Brain Sciences*, 6, 693-728

34. Dunham, P J (1972) Some effects of punishment on unpunished responding, *Journal of the Experimental Analysis of Behaviour*, 17, 443-450

35. Edwards, C A & Honig (1987) Memorization and 'feature selection' in the acquisition of natural concepts in pigeons, *Learning and Motivation*, 19, 235-260

36. Eisenberger, R, Pierce, W D & Cameron, J (1999) Effects of reward on intrinsic motivation – negative, neutral and positive, Comment on Deci, Koestner & Ryan, 1999, *Psychological Bulletin*, 125, 677-691

37. Ellard, M-E, & Crowell-Davis, (1989) Evaluating equine dominance in draft mares, *Applied Animal Behaviour Science*, 25, 55-75

38. Estes, W K & Skinner, B F (1941) Some quantitative properties of anxiety, *Journal of Experimental Psychology*, 29, 390-400

39. Fagen, R M & George, T K (1977) Play behaviour and exercise in young ponies (Equus caballus), *Behavioural Ecology and Sociobiology*, 2, 267-269

40. Fantino, E & Moore, J (1980) Uncertainty reduction, conditioned reinforcement and observing, *Journal of the Experimental Analysis of Behaviour*, 33, 3-13

41. Feh, C deMazieres (1993) Grooming at preferred site reduces heart rate in horses, *Animal Behaviour*, 46, 1191-1194

42. Feist, J D (1976) Behaviour patterns and communication in feral horses, *Zeitschrift fuer Tierpsychologie*, 41, 337-371

43. Ferster, C B & Skinner, B F (1957) *Schedules of reinforcement*, Appleton Century-Crofts, NY

44. Garcia, J & Koelling, R A (1966) The relation of cue to consequence in avoidance learning, *Psychonomic Science*, 4, 123-124

45. Gemberling, G A & Domjan, M (1982) Selective associations in one-day old rats: taste-toxicosis and texture-shock aversion learning, *Journal of Comparative and Physiological Psychology*, 96, 105-111

46. Gleitman, H (1971) Forgetting of long-term memeory in animals in Honig, W K & James, P H R (eds) *Animal memory*, Academic Press, USA

47. Grant, D S (1984) Rehearsal in pigeon short-term memory in Roitblat, H L Bever, T G & Terrace, H S (eds) *Animal cognition*, Erlbaum, NJ

48. Groves, P M & Thompson, R F (1971) Habituation: a dual process theory, *Psychological Review*, 77, 419-450

49. Haag, E L, Rudman, R & Houpt, K A (1980) Avoidance, maze learning and social dominance in ponies, *Journal of Animal Science*, 50, 329-335

50. Hall, G & Minor, H (1984) A search for context-stimulus associations in latent inhibition, Journal of Experimental Psychology: *Animal Behaviour Processes*, 5, 31-42

51. Hanggi, E B (1999) Interocular transfer of learning in horses, *Journal of Equine Veterinary Science*, 19, 518-523

52. Heird, J C, Lennon, A M & Bell, R W (1981) Effects of early experience on the learning ability of yearling horses,

REFERENCES

Journal of Animal Science, 53, 1204-1209

53. Heird, J C, Lokey, C E & Cogen, D C (1986) Repeatability and comparison of two maze tests to measure learning ability in horses, *Applied Animal Behaviour Science*, 16, 103-119

54. Heird, J C, Whitaker, D D, Bell, R W, Ramsey, C B & Lokey, C E (1986) The effects of handling at different ages on the subsequent learning ability of two-year-old horses, *Applied Animal Behaviour Science*, 15:15-25

55. Hearst, E (1968) Discrimination learning as the summation of excitation and inhibition, *Science*, 162, 1303-1306

56. Herrnstein, R J (1990) Rational choice theory: necessary but not sufficient, *American Psychologist*, 45, 356-367

57. Heth, D C (1976) Simultaneous and backward fear conditioning as a function of number of CS-UCS pairings, *Journal of Experimental Psychology: Animal Behaviour Processes*, 2, 117-129

58. Hoffman, H S (1969) Stimulus factors in conditioned suppression in Campbell, C A & Church, R M (eds) *Punishment and aversive behaviour*, Appleton Century-Crofts, NY

59. Hogan, E S, Houpt, K A & Sweeney, K (1988) The effects of enclosure size on social interactions and daily activity patterns of the captive Asiatic wild horse Equus Przewalski, *Applied Animal Behaviour Science,* 21, 147-168

60. Holland, J L, Kronfeld, D S & Meacham, T N (1996) Behaviour of horses is affected by soy lecithin and corn oil in the diet, *Journal of Animal Science,* 74, 1252-1255

61. Hollis, K L, Pharr, Dumas, M J, Britton, G B & Field, J (1997) Classical conditioning provides paternity advantage for territorial male blue gouramis (Trichogaster trichopterus), *Journal of Comparative Psychology*, 111, 219-225

62. Houpt, K A & Keiper, R (1982) The position of the stallion in the equine dominance hierarchy of feral and domestic ponies, *Journal of Animal Science*, 54, 945-950

63. Hunter, L & Houpt, K A (1989) Bedding material preferences of ponies, *Journal of Animal Science*, 67, 1986-1991

64. Ingold, T (1994) From trust to domination: an alternative history of human-animal relations in Manning, A & Serpell, J A (eds) *Animals and human society: changing perspectives*, 1-22, Routledge, London

65. Irwin, F W (1971) *Intentional behaviour and motivation: a cognitive theory*, Lippincott, USA

66. Jacobs, W J & Nadel, L (1985) Stress-induced recovery of fears and phobias, *Psychological Review*, 92, 512-531

67. Jezierski, T, Jaworski, Z & Gorecka, A (1999) Effects of handling on behaviour and heart rate of Konik horses: comparison of stable- and forest-reared youngstock, *Applied Animal Behaviour Science*, 62, 1-11

68. Joubert, E (1972) The social organisation and associated behaviour in the Hartmann zebra (Equus zebra hartmannae), *Madoqua Seriale* 1, 6, 17-56

69. Kagel, J H, Dwyer, G P & Battalio, R C (1985) Bliss points vs minimum needs: tests of competing motivational models, *Behavioural Processes*, 11, 61-77

70. Kamin, L J (1968) Predictability, surprise, attention and conditioning in Campbell, B A & Church (eds) *Punishment and aversive behaviour*, Appleton Century-Crofts, USA

71. Kamin, L J, Brimer, C J & Black, A H (1963) Conditioned suppression as a monitor of fear of the CS in the course of avoidance training, *Journal of Comparative and Physiological Psychology*, 56, 497-501

72. Kandel, E R (1991) Cellular mechanisms of learning and the biological basis of individuality in Kandel, E R Schwartz, J H & Jessell (Eds) *Principles of neural science*, Elsevier, NY

73. Keiper, R R & Keenan, M A (1980) Nocturnal activity patterns of feral ponies, *Journal of Mammology*, 61: 116-118

74. Klimov, A (1988) Spatial-ethological investigation of the herd of Przewalski horses in Askania-Nova, *Applied Animal Behaviour Science*, 21, 99-115

75. Kratzer, D D, Netherland, W M, Pulse, R E & Baker, J P (1977) Maze learning in quarter horses, *Journal of Animal Science*, 45, 896-902

76. Kusonose, R, Hatakeyama, H, Ischikawa, F, Kubo, K Kiguchi, A, Asai, Y & Ito, K (1986) Behavioural studies on yearling horses in field environments: effects of the group size on the behaviour of horses, *Bulletin of Equine Research Institute*, 23, 1-5

77. Kusonose, R, Hatakeyama, H, Ischikawa, F, A, Asai, Y & Ito, K (1987) Behavioural studies on yearling horses in field environments: effects of the pasture shape on the behaviour of horses, *Bulletin of Equine Research Institute*, 24, 1-5

78. Kusonose, R, Hatakeyama, H, Kubo, K Kiguchi, A, Asai, Y, Fujii, Y & Ito, K (1986) Behavioural studies on yearling horses in field environments: effects of the field size on the behaviour of horses, *Bulletin of Equine Research Institute*, 22, 1-7

79. Laudenslager, M L, Ryan, S M, Drugan, R C, Hyson, R L & Maier, S F (1983) Coping and immunosuppression: inescapable but not escapable shock suppresses lymphocyte proliferation, *Science*, 22, 568-570

80. Linklater, W L & Cameron, E Z (2000) Tests for co-operative behaviour between stallions, *Animal Behaviour*, 60, 731-743

81. Locurto, C, Terrace, H S & Gibbon, J (1976) Autoshaping, random control, and omission training in the rat, *Journal of the Experimental Analysis of Behaviour*, 26, 451-467

82. Mackintosh, N J (1974) *The psychology of animal learning*, Academic Press, NY

83. Maier, S F (1970) Failure to escape traumatic shock: incompatible skeletal motor responses or learned helplessness?, *Learning & Motivation*, 1, 157-170

84. Maier, S F & Seligman, M E P (1976) Learned helplessness: theory and evidence, *Journal of Experimental Psychology: General*, 105, 3-46

85. Mal, M E & McCall, C A (1996) The influence of handling during different ages on a halter leading training test in foals, *Applied Animal Behaviour Science*, 50, 115-120

86. Mal, M E, McCall, C A, Cummins, K A & Newland, M C (1994) Influence of preweaning handling methods on post-weaning learning ability and manageability of foals, *Applied Animal Behaviour Science*, 40, 187-195

87. Mayes, E & Duncan, P (1986) Temporal patterns of feeding in free-ranging horses, *Behaviour*, 96, 105-129

88. McCall, C A (1989) The effect of body condition of horses on discrimination learning abilities, *Applied Animal Behaviour Science*, 22, 327-334

89. McDonnell, S M & Poulin, A (2002) Equid play ethogram, *Applied Animal Behaviour Science*, 78, 263-290

90. McGreevy, P D, French, N P & Nicol, C J (1995) The prevalence of abnormal behaviours in dressage, eventing and endurance horses in relation to stabling, *Veterinary Record*, 137, 36-37

91. McGreevy, P D, Nicol, C J, Cripps, P, Green & French, N (1995) Management factors associated with stereotypic and redirected behaviour in the Thoroughbred horse, *Equine Veterinary Journal*, 27, 86-91

92. McGreevy, P D & Nicol, C J (1998) The effect of short-term prevention on the subsequent rate of crib-biting in Thoroughbred horses, *Equine Veterinary Journal*, 27, 30-35

93. McGreevy, P D & Nicol, C J (1998) Physiological and behavioural consequences associated with the prevention of crib-biting in horses, *Physiology of Behaviour*, 65, 15-23

94. Seligman, M E P (1968) Chronic fear produced by unpredictable shock, *Journal of Comparative and Physiological Psychology*, 66, 402-411

95. Maki, W S (1981) Directed forgetting in animals in Spear, N E & Miller, R R (eds) *Information processing in animals: memory mechanisms*, Erlbaum, NJ

96. Mills, D S, Eckley, S & Cooper, J J (2000) Thoroughbred bedding preferences, associated behaviour differences and their implications for equine welfare, *Animal Science*, 70, 95-106

97. Marks, I M (1972) Perspectives on flooding, *Seminars in Psychiatry*, 4, 129-138

98. Marlin, N A & Miller, R R (1981) Associations to contextual stimuli as a determinant of long-term habituation, *Journal of Experimental Psychology: animal behaviour processes*, 7, 313-333

99. McDowell, J J (1982) The importance of Herrnstein's mathematical formulation of the law of effect for behavioural therapy, *American Psychologist*, 37, 771-779

100. Mineka, S (1979) The role of fear in theories of avoidance learning, flooding and extinction, *Psychological Bulletin*, 86, 985-1010

101. Obrist, P A, Sutterer, J R & Howard, J L (1972) Preparatory cardiac changes: a psychobiological approach in Black, A H & Prokasy, W F (eds) *Classical conditioning II*, Appleton Century-Crofts, NY

102. Odberg, F O (1973) An interpretation of pawing by the horses (Equus caballus), displacement activity and original functions, *Saeugertieren*, 21, 1-12

103. Olds, M E & Fobes, J L (1981) The central basis of motivation: intracranial self-stimulation studies, *Annual Review of Psychology*, 32, 523-574

104. Pavlov, I (1927) *Conditioned reflexes*, Oxford University Press, UK

105. Premack, D (1978) On the abstractness of human concepts: why it would be difficult to talk to a pigeon in Hulse, S H, Fowler, H & Honig, W K (eds) *Cognitive processes in animal behaviour*, Erlbaum, NJ

106. Poplawski, L J & McCall, C A (1989) Developing a negative reinforcement avoidance learning test for horses, *Journal of Animal Science(suppl)*, 67, 95

107. Rescorla, R A & Heth, C D (1975) Reinstatement of fear to an extinguished conditioned stimulus, *Journal of Experimental Psychology: animal behaviour processes*, 1, 88-96

108. Riccio, D C & Silvestri (1973) Extinction of avoidance behaviour and the problem of residual fear, *Behaviour Research and Therapy*, 11, 1-9

109. Richardson, N R & Gratton, A (1996) Behaviour-relevant changes in nucleus accumbens dopamine transmission elicited by food reinforcement: an electrochemical study in rats, *Journal of Neuroscience*, 16, 8160-8169

110. Rifa, H (1990) Social facilitation in the horse (Equus caballus), *Applied Animal Behaviour Science*, 25, 167-176

111. Salter, R E & Hudson, R J (1979) Social organization of feral horses in Western Canada, *Applied Animal Behaviour Science*, 8, 207-223

112. Schilder, M B H, v Hoof, J A, v Geer-Plesman, C J & Wensing, J B (1984) A quantitative analysis of facial expression in the Plains Zebra, *Zeitschrift fuer Tierpsychologie*, 66, 11-32

113. Schultz, W (1998) Predictive reward signal of dopamine neurons, *Journal of Neurophysiology*, 80, 1-27

114. Seligman, M E P (1970) On the generality of laws of learning, *Psychological Review*, 77, 406-418

115. Sheffield, F D (1965) Relation between classical conditioning and instrumental learning in Prokasy, W F (ed) Classical conditioning, Appleton Century-Crofts, NY, *Journal of Experimental Psychology: Animal Behaviour Processes*,

116. Shermer, M (1999) *Why people believe weird things: pseudoscience, superstition and other confusions of our time*, Freeman, NY

117. Skinner, B F (1948) 'Superstition' in the pigeon, *Journal of Experimental Psychology*, 38, 168-172

118. Squire, L R & Kandel, E R (1999) *Memory: from mind to molecules*, Freeman, NY

119. Thomas, G V (1981) Contiguity, reinforcement rate and the law of effect, *Journal of Experimental Psychology*, 33B, 33-43

120. Thorndike, E L (1911) Animal intelligence: an experimental study of the associative processes in animals, *Psychological Monographs*, 2

121. Tilson, R L, Sweeney, K A, Binczik, G A & Reindl, N J (1988) Buddies and bullies: social structure of a bachelor group of Przewalski horses, *Applied Animal Behaviour Science*, 21, 169-185

122. Timberlake, W (1984) Behavioural regulation and learned performance: some misapprehensions and disagreements, *Journal of the Experimental Analysis of Behaviour*, 41, 355-375

123. Turner, J W & Morrison, M L (2001) Influence of predation by mountain lions on numbers and survivorship of a feral horse population, *Southwestern Nature*, 46, 183-190

124. Tyler, S J (1972) Behaviour and social organisation of semi-feral ponies, *Animal Behaviour Monograph*, 5

125. Wasserman, E A & Miller, R R (1997) What's elementary about associative learning? *Annual Review of Psychology*, 48, 573-607

126. Wells, S M v Goldschmidt-Rothschild, B (1979) Social behaviour and relationships in a herd of Camargue horses, *Zeitschrift fuer Tierpsychologie*, 49, 363-380

127. Wilson, C, Nomiko, G G, Collu, M & Fibiger, H C (1995) Dopaminergic correlates of behaviour: importance of drive, *Journal of Neuroscience*, 15, 5169-5178

128. Wolff, A & Hausberger, M (1996) Learning and memorisation of two different tasks in horses: the effects of age, sex and sire, *Applied Animal Behaviour Science*, 46, 137-143

129. Zanella, A J, Brunner, P, Unshelm, J, Mendl, M T & Broom, D M (1998) The relationship between housing and social rank on cortisol, endorphin and dynorphin 1-13 secretion in sows, *Applied Animal Behaviour Science*, 59, 1-10

130. Zeeb, K (1981) Basic behavioural needs of horses, *Applied Animal Ethology*, 7, 391-392

AUTHOR'S AKNOWLEDGEMENTS

From Thorndike, to Pavlov to Skinner, we have more than a century's worth of scientific analysis and understanding of how animals learn. From the works of early ethologists, such as Lorenz and Tinbergen, to dozens of modern-day equine behavioural scientists such as my own mentor, Professor Christine Nicol at Bristol Veterinary School, we have an abundance of scientific behavioural theory on which we can now rely.

To all these great theorists and scientists (and the countless others I do not have the space to mention individually), I acknowledge my debt in the creation of Teach Yourself Horse.

Karen Pryor too, deserves a special mention. Pryor became renowned in the 1960's for her work using positive reinforcement on dolphins, a species of animal that simply swims out of hearing if yelled at! Although not her invention, Pryor brought non-forceful clicker training for dogs and cats into the home and her video *Clicker Magic!* is a useful visual introduction to the clicker's application. Positive Horse Magic is an extension of her work – into the world of training horses.

Acknowledgements go also to the editorial team at D J Murphy and *Horse&Rider* magazine – Kate, Nicky, Jane, Janet, Alison and Danielle; each has played a significant role in getting Teach Yourself Horse into your hands.

I am grateful to Angela McCrickard, Tracey Hannan and Debbie de Sainte Croix for agreeing to allow me to share their stories of Inky, Ben and Kismet respectively (see Chapters 13, 14 and 15). Without their agreement, these cases would have remained confidential.

My family have earned my life-long gratitude too. My parents, Dr Ian and Jess McRae and my brother, Donald, have contributed to the growth and success of the Natural Animal Centre in ways that, until now, have never been publicly acknowledged. My parents, in particular, have spent hours reading long scripts on horse behaviour in efforts to formulate an opinion as to whether I have been successful at simplifying the science – thanks to you all.

To Ross, my husband and partner in life as well as horse training, my very special thanks and love for all your support for both the EBQ and the Teach Yourself Horse series. I would never have got here without you!

But perhaps my greatest debt is to all the horses and animals at the Natural Animal Centre who have taught me so much. From the chickens that were clicker-trained to wear nappies so they can visit me in the office, to giant rabbits that have learnt to nestle against the German Shepherd dogs for warmth and grooming, to horses that have put aside millions of years of fear and now lie down in the barn with the pigs – to all of these, I say thank you for the privilege of sharing your lives and for teaching me more about animals.

Heather Simpson

ABOUT THE AUTHOR

Born in South Africa, Heather Simpson's love of animals started at an early age and, as her long-suffering mother will testify, her bedroom was often a haven for all sorts of animals in need, from dogs to birds, fish – and even snakes! A teenage obsession revolved around frogs and, in particular, the unusual underwater-dwelling African Clawed Toad. She is especially proud of the fact that her toads began giving mating calls, even though it was thought at the time that this kind of amphibian would never breed in captivity! Management of animals in a domestic setting is thus not a new line of thought for her.

Heather graduated from the University of South Africa with a Masters degree and then completed further post-graduate animal behaviour science at Southampton University. She is currently working on her doctorate on how horses accomplish advanced types of learning.

Although she spends most of her time at the Natural Animal Centre in Wales, Heather is passionate about wildlife and makes several trips a year to countries like Zambia, Botswana, Namibia and South Africa to study the behaviour of the Plains zebra, a much neglected species from a behavioural science research point of view. She intends to publish her scientific findings within the next couple of years.

Heather's other book, *Emotional Health for Horses*, was co-authored with Stefan Ball and Judy Howard, and is about treating emotional problems in horses with Bach Flower Remedies. Heather is currently the only lecturer endorsed by the Dr Edward Bach Foundation to teach the Accredited Certification for Animal Practitioners.

When she is not working, Heather loves taking her dogs and horses for some fun on the beach.

133